S0-AEU-360

Blessed Are the Debonair

*

BOOKS BY *Margaret Case Harriman*

TAKE THEM UP TENDERLY

THE VICIOUS CIRCLE

BLESSED ARE THE DEBONAIR

*

BLESSED
ARE
THE
DEBONAIR

*

by Margaret Case Harriman

ILLUSTRATED BY *Mircea Vasiliu*

*

Rinehart & Company, Inc.
NEW YORK
TORONTO

Grateful acknowledgment is made to the following publishers for permission to use excerpts from their copyrighted publications:

F. B. Haviland Publishing Company, 112 West 44th Street, New York 36, N. Y., for permission to reprint brief lyrics from "Lam', Lam', Lam'" by Frank Abbott.

The Macmillan Company, New York, N. Y., for permission to reprint four lines from "The Song of the Wandering Aengus" from COLLECTED POEMS, by William Butler Yeats, copyright, 1906, 1934, by The Macmillan Company.

Music Publishers Holding Corporation, New York, N. Y., for permission to reprint an excerpt from the lyrics of "Swanee," copyright, 1919, and copyright renewed, by New World Music Corporation.

G. Schirmer, Inc., New York, N. Y., copyright owners and publishers, for permission to reprint two lines from "Will You Remember" from MAYTIME, by Sigmund Romberg.

The book referred to in the second paragraph on page 205 is "Ross and *The New Yorker*" by Dale Kramer. Doubleday, 1951.

Published simultaneously in Canada by Clarke, Irwin & Company, Ltd., Toronto

© 1956 by Margaret Case Harriman

Illustrations © 1956 by Rinehart & Company, Inc.

Printed in the United States of America

All Rights Reserved

Library of Congress Catalog Card Number: 56–7255

Heureux les débonnaires
cars ils hériteront la terre.
—FRENCH BIBLE, MATTHEW 5:5

* Foreword *

READERS do not care why a book is written. For them it is simply *there*, like the breakfast marmalade or Jackie Gleason on television, to be considered or ignored; and that is as it should be.

Nevertheless, although my publishers suggested this book some time ago, it would probably never have been written had it not been for a curious experience I had in a Spanish forest last year.

I had taken a sight-seeing bus from Madrid to Segovia to see the palace of Philip IV of Spain at La Granja, and upon arrival the busload was separated as usual into English-speaking, French-speaking, and Spanish-speaking groups. I followed the French group, which looked the most interesting. As we proceeded into a marble courtyard I was surprised to hear an extremely British masculine voice in my ear, inquiring, "I say, do you speak English?"

The fact of an Englishman, any Englishman, speaking to any stranger in public so astonished me that I stammered, in English but making no sense whatever, "No, I speak French, but I'm American."

This lunacy so diverted Ivor, which turned out to be the

Englishman's name, that we spent the rest of the day together.

"Let's get out of this chamber of horrors," said Ivor when we were inside the palace and a glance had satisfied us that it was furnished in a bastard profusion of Irish-lace curtains and Japanese-lacquered tables. So we eluded the guides and the other trippers and went to walk in the park.

The park at La Granja is a part of the forest where Philip IV hunted with his queen and his court, and the minute you stepped onto its formal paths you got the feeling of hunting horns and plumes—as though a royal company, dashing and debonair, might come galloping around any corner. It was a bright October day with the trees scarlet and bronze against a sky of blazing blue, and the leaves rustled underfoot as we walked along the path, which now began to wind steeply upward.

"I'll bet you ten shillings I know what's at the top of this hill," said Ivor as we climbed.

"No fair. You've been here before."

"I haven't, I swear it. Will you bet?"

"Oh well, okay. I bet it's a ravine, or a gully with a railroad track running through it."

"You have no romance," Ivor snorted. "*I* bet it's a lake."

"Ho! How can you have a lake at the top of a hill?" I scoffed, and recalled too late that Spanish kings in the seventeenth century could have almost anything almost anywhere they liked.

We reached the top of the hill . . . and I don't think I ever even remembered to pay Ivor his ten shillings. Before us, secret and serene as one of the waters of the moon, was a tiny lake, heavenly blue except where it reflected the brilliance of the trees around it. On its opposite shore stood a little pink and white chalet with a solid gold tree beside it, and the pink and white and the solid gold were repeated in the still blue water of the lake.

There wasn't another human being there to see it. There wasn't a sound anywhere, except the occasional whisper of a falling leaf. Ivor and I sat down on a convenient stone bench (trust those Spanish kings for convenience), and we didn't speak or even smoke a cigarette. We just filled our eyes with this lovely surprise the forest had given us.

Even now, I can close my eyes and see it. I forget a little what Ivor looks like, although he has become a good friend and comes to see me whenever he is in New York. I am a little hazy about the glories of the Blue Grotto at Capri, and about the Grand Canyon, and Mont-Saint-Michel, and other wonders I have beheld. But at night sometimes, if I have trouble going to sleep, I can close my eyes and see that magic lake at La Granja reflecting its pink and white chalet and its solid gold tree, and I can hear its stillness.

I am not sure how long we sat there, and we were rather quiet walking back to the palace. Suddenly, in a clearing in the forest, I stood rock-still. A figure stood before me that was not of the ghostly royal company, and yet had a debonair bearing of its own. I stared . . . a sunbeam flickered . . . and he was gone.

"What was it?" Ivor asked anxiously as we went on again. "You went white as a sheet."

"Oh, nothing," I said. "Except . . . do you know, all at once I *saw* my father standing in that clearing? He died in nineteen forty-six, and I saw him there as clearly as I see you."

"Well, of course you did," said Ivor comfortably. "Don't you know that when you are in a very quiet place, in a forest or by the sea, someone you loved is very likely to be with you there? I should have thought a big girl like you would have known that by this time. Now, do come on," said Ivor, tucking my hand under his elbow and patting it, "we'd better get back to the trippers or that guide *will* start creating."

In the bus going back to Madrid, he asked, "By the way, who was your father?"

"His name was Frank Case, and he owned the Algonquin Hotel in New York."

Ivor bounced around on the seat and gazed at me in astonishment. "Frank Case of the Algonquin! I *say!* Was he really your father?"

"Yes, did you know him?"

"No, but all of my friends knew him and I've heard all about him, of course. Everybody knows about Frank Case of the Algonquin. I say!" Ivor went on. "You must know Constance Collier and Leslie Banks and Dennis King, and all that crew. . . ."

Well, there it was again. It happens all the time, in one way or another. Here was I, three thousand miles from home, among the mountains of Spain, and an Englishman whom I had never seen two hours earlier was saying, "But of course I know all about Frank Case of the Algonquin! We knew absolutely *all* the same people. . . . By jove, this is positively splendid!"

At my hotel in Madrid a cable was waiting from my publishers in New York. "What about that book you were going to write about your father and you?" it inquired.

"Nothing simpler," I cabled back blithely, "just saw Father today."

Blessed Are the Debonair

* Chapter 1 *

IN the lobby of the Algonquin Hotel on West Forty-fourth Street two clocks, situated in a manner which I can only describe as askance from each other, have carried on a kind of cockeyed warfare for over forty years that I personally remember. One is the Western Union clock over the front desk, a square-faced timepiece, accurate to the split-second and rather fussy about it. The other is a grandfather's clock which stands, tall and confident, in a niche halfway across the room, leering faintly at Western Union and (I swear) deliberately spacing its deep quarter-hour chimes a few seconds before or after the electrical precision of its squat-faced rival.

If ever a clock had a right to tell time in its own way, I suppose it is this grandfather's clock. Authority has it that the Western Union affair is an upstart of only some forty-five years ago, and that the grandfather's clock has tolled the hours in the Algonquin lobby for over fifty years. Certainly the grandfather's clock has a more commanding presence than Old Squat-face, and people pay more attention to it, right or wrong.

Actors and actresses hurrying from the dining room on

their way to work always consult it as they go by, and it has known half a century of them. Mrs. Fiske, darting and feminine, perhaps escorted by a youthful Alexander Woollcott; John Drew and the Barrymores, elegant and composed; the acrobatic Douglas Fairbanks and the equally agile Elsie Janis; the suave set, including Gertrude Lawrence, Beatrice Lillie, Noel Coward and Leslie Howard; and on and on (one is tempted to go *tick-tock* at this point) through Helen Hayes, Humphrey Bogart, Shirley Booth and Mary Martin. To name a few.

Playwrights, hating to go back to work after lunch at the Algonquin Round Table, have been stirred to action by its warning bong. Among them were Robert Sherwood, George Kaufman, Marc Connelly and Maxwell Anderson. Other writers at the Round Table heard the warning too, but being writers, often happily ignored it beyond asking a waiter to sharpen a pencil, just in case. "I might need that someday," Bob Benchley once observed, tucking the sharpened pencil into his waistcoat pocket and leaning back to enjoy some more good talk.

On opening nights, drama critics—George Jean Nathan, Dick Watts, Wolcott Gibbs and the rest—generally scurried out after the actors in more ways than one, and seldom without a glance at the grandfather's clock to tell them how much time they had to see the show, write the review, and go comfortably home to Bleeck's, an all-night tavern dear to their hearts.

In spite of Western Union's accuracy staring them in the face, practically everybody in the Algonquin kept time by the grandfather's clock. My father, Frank Case, was a stickler for punctuality, yet he never set his own watch, a thin gold pocket number, by any other authority. Somehow it seemed that the old clock belonged there, and was a part of the Algonquin's tradition. And if you doubt the force of the Algonquin's tradition, remember that Englishman I met in the mountains of Spain who knew all about it.

As for me, I grew up under the grandfather's clock without being much aware of it until, one evening, it handed me a shock. I must have been about eight years old. Father and I happened to be sitting on a couch facing the grandfather's clock when it chimed the half-hour: half past six.

"Father," I said, "did you ever realize that it will never again be half past six on March thirty-first, nineteen hundred and fourteen?"

It was my first intimation of mortality.

Father enjoyed these random thoughts in the young, but he was the first to put his foot down on any overprecociousness. He never let me forget another childlike remark I made a year or so later.

Mr. and Mrs. John Drew lived in the Algonquin. Mr. Drew was, of course, the Beau Brummel of the American stage, and Mrs. Drew was a gentle, white-haired lady, beloved by all. There was nobody, from an Algonquin bellboy to a British Queen, who did not love and admire Mrs. Drew. One evening, Mr. and Mrs. Drew stepped out of the Algonquin elevator on the way to some party, and they made so handsome a couple that every eye in the lobby followed them out of the front door, including Father's and mine.

"You know," I said, turning earnestly to Father, "I *like* Mrs. Drew!"

Father eyed me with considerable humor. "That's mighty tolerant of you," he allowed.

For years afterward, whenever I ventured the opinion that Ernest Hemingway wrote well, or that Katharine

Cornell was a good actress, Father would give me the old eagle eye and murmur, " 'I *like* Mrs. Drew.' " He was a hard man in some ways, my father.

My "liking" of Mrs. Drew was spontaneous—I never knew her very well—but I had a more realistic attachment to Mrs. William Collier, who also lived in the Algonk with her husband, a famous comedian, and their son, "Buster" Collier. On cold winter days Mrs. Collier used to ask me to her apartment, and always gave me a great steaming mug of hot malted milk, made out of Horlick's tablets which she kept in the bookcase and a bottle of milk kept on the fire escape, the whole thing heated up on an electric grill.

Mrs. Collier's malted milk remains in my mind as the greatest "treat" of my childhood. And that is strange, because, as the innkeeper's daughter, I could order practically anything I wanted from the hotel menu. Every day, I could have any kind of five soups, any kind of meat from lamb chops to filet mignon, any of eight or ten vegetables, and all the ice cream and cake I could hold.

But it all appeared automatically, from chefs in the kitchen whom I had never seen. I think the reason I loved Mrs. Collier's hot malted milk was because it was the first time I had ever seen anyone cook something especially for *me*.

The reader will gather from the above that I was not only a hotel child, but a motherless hotel child. I had better go back and explain this a little.

My father and mother, Frank and Caroline Case, left their home town, Buffalo, around the turn of the century and came to New York to crack the big town wide open. They were young and gay and debonair, and the big town slapped them in the face. They wound up in Jersey City, where Father got a job as night clerk at Taylor's Hotel. He was fired from there for roller skating in the lobby to keep himself awake.

"This," said Frank, "is where we move on to New York."

"I'm ready," said Caroline, gay and pregnant.

They moved to a hall bedroom in the west forties, and ate mostly eggs boiled over the gas burner while Frank looked for a job. They had a child, stillborn, but carefully christened Francis Manning Case III.

One day Frank, in search of a job, wandered along Forty-fourth Street and noticed a new building going up. He went in and asked for a job.

"What can you do?" asked the boss.

"Anything! Everything!" said Frank desperately.

So he was hired, at the new Algonquin, in exactly that capacity; he was renting agent, desk clerk, night watchman, and trouble shooter for anything that came along. Mr. Foster, the boss, made one concession: since Frank Case had to be on duty eighteen hours a day, and since he was a family man, he and his wife could have a room in the hotel and two meals a day.

Caroline moved joyfully into 1206 and, after a steak dinner one night, jovially gave birth to me. I have this only from Father, of course, who said Mother was never happier and demanded another steak and a glass of beer ten minutes after I was born.

Father always said that it was my mother's gaiety and charm that lured the first customers into the Algonquin, and he was supported by many of Mother's friends, including Charles Hanson Towne and Frank Crowninshield. "Caroline had golden hair and violet-colored eyes," said Charley Towne, perhaps with a poet's license, "and how she could *sing*, in that glorious contralto!"

Crowny was crisper. "What a pity you don't resemble your mother, you lean wretch," he once remarked, regarding me over his pince-nez.

Both Father and Mother had youth and the gift of laughter, and even in the hall-bedroom days managed to find life pretty humorous. On one of their anniversaries, Father used to recall, he decided that they would dress up and he would take Mother out to dine at Shanley's, the Stork Club of the period.

"I know what I want," said Mother as they sat down in the glittering palace. "I'd like to have an artichoke because I've never tasted one."

"Neither have I. We will both have artichokes!" Father said grandly.

Artichokes cost two dollars apiece, even then, so artichokes were *all* they had for dinner, and an artichoke can be terribly unrewarding when served as the main and only dish.

"I'm glad we had these," said Mother happily, when she had finished scraping away at the bristly delicacy. "Now I know one thing I don't want any *of* when we get rich."

Father always felt comforted that he had been able to give Mother a few good things before the end of her short lifetime. I have a zircon ring surrounded by diamonds, a gold owl's-head pin with diamond eyes, and a French clock that he gave her, and also another jewelled trinket which she came by in a more colorful way. This is a ten-dollar gold piece made into a brooch and heavily encrusted with the initials "P.D. Jr." in diamonds. It was some time after Father gave me this brooch that I heard the true story of it. It seems that Mother had been engaged to Peter Doelger Jr., the brewer's son, and when she broke the engagement to marry Father she returned Peter's ring but declined to return his initialed brooch, giving the sound reason that she had taken it away from him in the first place because he insisted on wearing it as a scarfpin. "I simply couldn't have a man I was once even slightly engaged to going around with diamonds all over his chest," she explained. Mr. Doelger's loss was my gain, and his staggering scarfpin makes a handsome clip.

Mother apparently had a spirited way of removing clutter from other people's lives. One day she took me to call on a young actress named Leona Anderson, who lived in the hotel (her brother was Bronco Billy Anderson, the first of the movie cowboys), and spied a great white Teddy bear sitting on the piano. Teddy bears were the smart accessory for young women in those days.

"If there is one thing I consider tacky, it's a grown woman horsing around with a Teddy bear," said Mother, according to Miss Anderson who still likes to recall this incident. "Why don't you give your horrid toy to Margaret?"

Miss Anderson helplessly gave me the Teddy bear and a long time afterward, after Mother had died, somebody christened him Maximilian. Leona Anderson claims that Father named him after her brother, Bronco Billy, whose real name was G. Maximilian Aaronson, but I am inclined to doubt that. Father was always punctilious, and I think that if he had ever intended to name a Teddy bear after a man called G. Maximilian Aaronson he would have formally christened the bear G. Maximilian Aaronson and would, furthermore, have insisted that the bear be addressed as G. Maximilian Aaronson. As far as I know, my Teddy bear never had a surname. He was just known as Maxie.

Maxie, having joined the Case family, entered into a life that was pure hell. My brother gave him a hot bath and a haircut from which he never recovered. I left him, one summer day, in a field where some animal chewed off his right arm. This bit of carelessness led to one of those family sayings that continue through the years.

Father and the Algonquin were doing better then, and we had a car and a chauffeur named Albert. Albert was a boy ambitious for culture, who never used a plain word where a fancy one would do. He found Maxie, wounded in the field, and brought him back to me at arm's length.

"I fear," said Albert, "that one of its members is missing."

That simple sentence, one of the simplest Albert ever spoke, became in time a kind of signal between Father and me. Whenever we came up against something vexing —a bad book, or a dull guest, or a cough in a boat engine —one of us would murmur, "I fear . . ." and the other would finish the sentence in his mind. Later we were able to elaborate on it.

Father took me to the opening night of a play in which the hero, an actor named Montague Love, rescued the colonel's daughter from maddened natives and, amid a hail of poisoned spears, carried her to shelter in his own hut. With weapons flying past his head and the natives outside setting fire to the hut, he placed her in a chair and tenderly spoke these words:

"May I fetch you—a stimulant?"

After that, Father and I developed a double signal in time of stress or strain.

Vasiliu

FATHER: "I fear—that one of its members is missing."
ME: "May I fetch you—a stimulant?"

Few people heard us, and nobody knew what we were talking about, but we enjoyed it. There is nothing more satisfying than a private family code.

"Especially between a couple of screwballs," remarks Maxie who now, some forty years older and dirtier and with another foot and an eye gone, is draped on a couch across the room and regarding me out of his remaining eye as I write this.

My mother, Caroline, died when my brother Carroll was born and when I was too young to remember her well. My only distinct memory of her came to me accidentally twenty years after she was dead. I was reading my son to sleep with Robert Louis Stevenson's "A Child's Garden of Verses":

> *In winter I get up at night,*
> *And dress by yellow candle-light . . .*

Suddenly a tune, a melody which I never remembered hearing, came into my mind. "Hey, this is a song!" I informed my sleepy child, and I sang the rest of it to him:

> *In* SUM-*mer, quite the other way,*
> *I* HAF *to go to bed by* DAY . . .

I finished the whole song, right down to the end:

> *And does it not seem* HARD *to you,*
> *When all the sky is* BRIGHT *and blue,*
> *And I should like so much to play,*
> *To* HAF *to go to bed . . . by day?*

As I got up to leave the nursery, I ran into Father standing in the doorway. He was dining with us that night. He pulled me into the hall and gently closed the nursery door.

"Where did you ever learn that song?" he demanded.

"I don't know," I said vaguely, "it just came to me. I think maybe Mother used to sing it to me."

"She did," said Father. "She *did*." Whereupon he gave me a great hug and we proceeded arm in arm down the hall to join the company in the living room.

I have always been glad that, if I can have only one memory of my mother, it's the memory of a song.

During the eight years that Father remained a widower, I suppose no two children ever had a nursery so crowded with beautiful actresses tucking them in bed as my brother Carroll and I did. Some of them were just motherly, I guess, but I bet that some were not. After all, Father was young, attractive, increasingly prosperous, and unattached. Some of those actresses fair *smothered* us kids with attention.

I remember mainly Jane Grey and Jane Cowl, because they were the prettiest.

One night Father came into the bathroom while I was having my bath, and said, "Margaret, I think I would like to marry Jane. Is it all right with you?"

"No," I said sullenly.

"But why not?" asked Father, perching on the edge of the tub. "She loves you and Carroll, and she loves me, and she will make a *home* for us. We need that."

"No," I said stubbornly.

"All right, darling," said Father. He patted me on the

head, stood up, and turned in the doorway. "I still can't understand," he said, *"why* you don't want me to marry Jane."

I burst into great sobs and blubbered, "I don't know *which* Jane you *mean!"*

Possibly owing to my strong feelings in the bathtub (and no doubt for other reasons as well) Father remained single, and Carroll and I remained the petted darlings of the Algonk. Carroll, still a baby with a trained nurse, was not active socially; but I, as Father's daughter and a motherless child, came in for a good deal of attention. Rose Stahl, the beloved star of *The Chorus Lady* and *Maggie Pepper,* gave me a long gold chain with a tiny gold mesh purse at the end of it; William Hodge, famous as "The Man from Home" in the play by Booth Tarkington and Harry Leon Wilson, waited nightly to drink his after-dinner coffee until I was allowed to stop by his table on my way to bed and put a lump of sugar in it. Richard Harding Davis gave me a dispatch case he had carried through foreign wars. Irvin S. Cobb inscribed his book "Speaking of Operations" for me: "To my small friend Miss Margaret Case, from her large friend, Irvin S. Cobb." John Drew, Raymond Hitchcock and his wife, Flora Zabelle, and the first Mrs. Douglas Fairbanks (now Mrs. Jack Whiting) gave me other books, acres of them, which I still have and still read: "The Water Babies," "Tanglewood Tales," "The Secret Garden," "Sara Crewe," "Little Women," "Alice," and all of Robert Louis Stevenson, to name just a few. Frank Ward O'Malley, the star reporter of the *Sun* started me on the "Little Colonel" books with a Christmas gift, one year, of "The Little Colonel's House-party" inscribed in his beautiful pen-and-ink script:

"Let me say in this, now, space,
"My heart's yours to tally.
"A merry Christmas, Margaret Case,
"From old Frank Ward O'Malley."

It was one of my treasured "Little Colonel" books that led to my first misunderstanding with Father.

Standing in the middle of the living room one Christmas after we had opened our presents, he surveyed the tables and couches overflowing with gifts from Algonquin guests and shook his head. "It's too much," he murmured, "too much for just two children." Then he added cheerfully to me, "But anyway, you had a wonderful Christmas, didn't you? You certainly got everything you could have wanted, and more besides!"

"No," I said mournfully.

"What!" Father exclaimed. "What more could you possibly want?"

"I wanted some pearls," I told him. "Some white pearls and some black pearls."

Father stared. "Black pearls, forsooth!"

"She's terribly spoiled," said Jenkie, the nurse, coming in and overhearing. "Come on, Miss Millions, you'll take your nap."

"Yes, put her to bed," said Father, grimly. "I'm only sorry it hasn't got spikes in it."

For some tongue-tied reason I could never tell Father that what I wanted the "pearls" for was to make a necklace like the one Lloyd Sherman, "The Little Colonel," made, with a white pearl bead to mark the days when she had been good and a black pearl bead for the days when she was bad. The exalted moment passed, and I went on being

26

good and bad with no black and white pearl necklace to signify the difference. With nothing to signify the difference, in fact, except Father's eyebrows.

Father had a way of cocking his right eyebrow at you that could make you suddenly conscious that you were lacking in charm. One day, some years after the pearl-necklace incident, I came breezing home with the Gardner School Yearbook in which I had been voted the Prettiest and the Cleverest girl in school. Father smiled and nodded agreement, but when I rather loudly complained that, since I had been voted the Cleverest, I saw no reason why Olga Gennert should have been voted the Most Intelligent, he cocked an eyebrow and came at me with Shakespeare, which was always at the tip of his tongue.

" 'Lay not that flattering unction to your soul,' " he advised. Then he went on to explain the difference between intelligence and mere cleverness, with a rider to the effect that the former was far more to be desired. However, when he read on down the list and found that a girl named LaRuna Wolcott had been voted Best Dancer, he cocked an eyebrow again and said, "Why weren't *you* voted Best Dancer?"

I knew what he meant. I had had enough practice, goodness knows. Father and I had always danced together, whenever anybody started a phonograph record or a pianola roll. What's more, I had danced at the age of nine with the nation's number-one waltzer, Donald Brian, who had been only a few years earlier the original "Prince Danilo" in the first New York production of *The Merry Widow*. I shall always remember my waltz with Donald Brian. He looked into my eyes the entire time, and I realize now how difficult this must have been for him, since my head came only to his third vest button.

Our waltz—Mr. Brian's and mine—occurred at a party I was allowed to attend by special permission from Father. Father was a great one for parties, especially dances, and there were always one or two a month going on in the Algonquin when I was a child. They were held in an apartment annex to the hotel, one flight up and affectionately known as "The Tomps' Apartment." The name derived from the fact that the apartment, including a large ballroom, had once been leased to Fred Thompson who owned Luna Park, and the secondary fact that I, dimly aware of its wonders, couldn't pronounce "Thompson." I called it "the Tomps' Apartment" and the name caught on. This was at a time when the turkey trot and even the one-step were barred from public dance floors, and the respectable but dance-mad residents of the Algonk—Father, Mr. and Mrs. Hitchcock, Mr. and Mrs. Drew, Mr. and Mrs. Fairbanks, Mr. and Mrs. Arnold Daly, and so on—decided to give their own dances in the Tomps' Apartment. Father has told in his book, "Tales of a Wayward Inn," how this group expanded into the famous Sixty Club, and later into the Embassy Club.

I was too young to go to the parties in the Tomps' Apartment. I heard everybody talking about them, I saw Father arrayed in white tie and tails ready to take off; I could even, lying in my little bed, faintly hear the rhythm of the music. Once, from my bedroom window, I saw some men pushing a couple of giant marimbas across Forty-fourth Street from the Hippodrome to the Algonquin; they had been borrowed from a marimba band then playing at the Hippodrome to lend novelty to the orches-

tra playing for that night's ball. I must have uttered some
lament about being left out of these festivities because,
when a Tomps' Apartment masquerade ball coincided
with my ninth birthday, Father said I could go for an
hour.

"You can wear a costume and a mask, so nobody will
recognize you and think I'm crazy," he said.

Fate played madly into my hands. Ann Pennington,
then a star of the Ziegfeld Follies, asked Father if she
could borrow some of my clothes to wear to the masquerade; she planned to go as a little girl.

"Why, of course!" said Father. "And Margaret can borrow *your* clothes and go as Ann Pennington, and nobody
will be able to tell you apart! It's a pretty cute idea, don't
you think?"

"Well . . ." said Miss Pennington.

Miss Pennington was provided with a white piqué dress
of mine, my pink sash, white socks, and black patent-
leather strap-slippers, all of which fitted her to perfection.
She had long hair hanging to her waist, just as I had, and
she tied a pink ribbon around her head, just as I did. She
had, moreover, her famous dimpled knees. She didn't look
a day over ten.

Encouraged by this perfect form-fit, Father and Miss
Pennington helped me into a costume of hers. It had se-
quins and feathers on it, to my great excitement, and I
stuck out my chest and wiggled my hips like a Follies
girl. I thought I was great until I caught Father's stricken
gaze.

"Get out of that thing!" he shouted. "You look thirty,
if you look a day!"

Ann Pennington went to the masquerade party in my

29

clothes, and was the belle of the ball. I went to the party
—after some rummaging by Jenkie among red and green
flannel—as Little Red Riding Hood.

But I had a good time, too. I waltzed with Donald
Brian, who looked right into my eyes.

* Chapter 2 *

IN 1916, Father, who was never immune to actresses except matrimonially, married Bertha Walden who was a non-actress in contrast to the two Janes, and a cool blonde in contrast to Caroline, who was a warm blonde. Bertha became immediately and forever known to us as "Bud"—a nickname my brother gave her—and, for the thirty years more that she lived, gave us kids the reassuring presence of one of the happiest marriages I have ever known.

The wedding had its colorful aspects. It took place at the Cathedral of St. John the Divine which was still under construction at Amsterdam Avenue and One Hundred and Twelfth Street, and had scaffolding all over its walls and most of its entrances. Bishop Burch performed the ceremony, and Douglas Fairbanks was Father's best man.

Fifteen minutes before the ceremony was scheduled to begin, the best man had not yet arrived. The guests began moving nervously in their pews. Father, in the vestry, cast anguished looks at the bishop. Nobody knows what the bride was going through. Ten minutes before the cere-

mony—still no best man. *Seven* minutes . . *five* min.
utes.

Suddenly everybody became aware of a familiar sound
they had been hearing for some time outside the church.
It was the occasional roar of the muffler cut-out on a
Stutz Bearcat as it passed, dwindled, and then returned.
Father and Bishop Burch rushed to a window, and sure
enough, there was Mr. Fairbanks racing around the Cathe-
dral in a puzzled way. They waved and shouted, and Mr.
Fairbanks waved and shouted back.

"I can't get *in!*" he yelled. "I've been around this church
ten times, and the doors are all boarded UP!"

"This way!" shouted Bishop Burch, pointing downward
through the scaffolding to a door that had been left open for
the wedding. "*This* way!"

"*This* way, Doug!" Father howled, also pointing.

"Oh, *that* way!" said Mr. Fairbanks, getting out of his
car. And, naturally, he climbed the scaffolding and came
in by way of the same open, stained-glass window Father
and the Bishop had been shouting from.

Once on deck, he was the perfect best man, proper as
anything in morning coat and striped trousers, and he
produced the ring promptly. I venture to say he was the
calmest person present.

Bud, however, was so unnerved that when John Purroy
Mitchell, then Mayor of New York, and some other notables proposed a toast to her later on at the wedding breakfast at the Algonquin, she stood up and drank her own
health three times before she came back to consciousness.

Perhaps I ought to give, at this point, some background
of the people I have been writing about: my mother, my
father and my stepmother.

I don't know much about my mother, except that her parents owned a hotel at Niagara Falls, and she was a well-known concert and choir singer in Buffalo. Flossie Young, her niece and my cousin, sometimes talks about her when we sit together on the terrace of her home in East Aurora. "Aunt Carrie's Christmas box was the big thing in my life," Flossie remembers. "We were poor, and *she* was poor, but she always sent exactly what I wanted. And of course you remember," Flossie chuckles, "the famous thing about your Aunt Millie and your Aunt Pansy?"

No, I don't remember. I remember Aunt Millie, all right. She was Flossie's mother, and Caroline's sister, and I spent many wonderful days at her house on Lafayette Avenue. Aunt Millie, like my mother, was born an Eckert, and she had the German love of cooking. The kitchen was the center of her house, and the most marvelous smells came out of it regularly: chili sauce, noodles, strudels, and grape jelly are the ones I remember. I even remember Aunt Millie draping some kind of noodles over the backs of kitchen chairs and warning me not to touch them until they "took shape." This sounds unlikely, but Flossie tells me that I could be right.

Aunt Pansy, on the other hand, was my father's sister and was rather grand, like most of the Cases. No smells ever came out of *her* kitchen, you can bet your life. It took me many years to appreciate Aunt Pansy, and to recognize that she is the feminine counterpart of my father—stern, skeptical and humorous, and full of affection, too. Certainly I never placed her in my mind along with jolly, easygoing, strudel-making Aunt Millie. I said as much to Flossie.

"Well, you're crazy, they were the greatest friends," said

Floss. And then she told me the famous story about the time Father invited them both to New York, for a visit at the Algonquin. Aunt Millie has been dead for many years, but I checked this tale only last week with Aunt Pansy who, at seventy-three, is still grand, humorous and altogether lovely.

It seems the girls drove from Buffalo to New York in a Model-T Ford, supplied with a lunch from a friendly neighbor which consisted of two cold broiled guinea hens and a bottle of gin. From time to time they refreshed themselves along the way, and finally, some thirty miles from Manhattan, drew up at the side of the road and went to sleep. Hale and hearty with the morning sun, they proceeded to Manhattan and the Algonquin, where they were met by Father, who had been calling Buffalo all night and was jumping up and down.

"We merely wish to sleep," the girls informed him. "Kindly show us to our room."

Father kindly showed them to their room and left them alone, for the time being. He had many other things on his mind. He was only the manager of the Algonquin then, he didn't want any relatives raising a ruckus, and besides, he had a new customer, a Mrs. Deems, who showed encouraging signs of eating large meals in her room.

That evening, he personally accompanied Mrs. Deems's dinner upstairs in the service elevator, noting with satisfaction the number of silver-covered dishes on the service table, and the discreet little check peeping out from under one of them and amounting to ten dollars plus. Almost purring, he followed the waiter out of the elevator and to the door of the apartment.

"Wait! This isn't Mrs. Deems's apartment!" he cried.

"No, sir," said the waiter, "this dinner is for your sister

and your sister-in-law. The check, you will see, is marked 'Complimentary.' "

I note that I have digressed, as I always do when enticed by an anecdote. I started out to tell something of the backgrounds of my mother, my father, and my stepmother, Bud.

I don't know much about Bud's actually. She was born in Albany, and her mother took in sewing to send her to school. Many years later, when Peyton Van Rensselaer came to live at the Algonquin, Bud won his enduring friendship by saying to him candidly, "I was born in Rensselaer County, but I never thought I would grow up to meet a real, live, Van Rensselaer." She and Mr. Van Rensselaer, a handsome man with white hair and a white goatee, shared an enthusiasm for eighteenth-century English furniture and early-American glass, and one of the endearing things about Bud was that she never got over the wonder of a real, live, Van Rensselaer asking her opinion about a Sheraton secretary, or a piece of Bristol glass, or a silver-luster creamer.

My father's people go back to the War of the Revolution, to one Benjamin Case who "went to Boston from Coventry in the Lexington Alarm list of 1775 and served two days as Sergeant." I once asked Aunt Pansy about this. "Why one small sergeant who served two lousy days?" I inquired. "Why couldn't we have had a general or something?"

"Oh, we had generals," said Pansy calmly. "In fact we had *two* generals in the War of the Revolution."

"Well, why don't we trace our ancestry back to *them?*" I demanded. "Why this one small sergeant who served *two days* in the Lexington Alarm?"

"Because," Pans told me with some severity, "the Lexington Alarm was the noblest moment of the Revolutionary War. Besides," she added peacefully, "Benjamin was the only one who stayed alive and had children."

Sergeant Benjie, God bless him, had plenty of children and I am enchanted by their names, sent to me long ago on a D.A.R. application form. Benjamin Case married Abigail Richardson in 1775, and their sons were Squire, Tubal and Arial Manning. Arial Manning Case married Lucy Hall in 1796 and they produced Abel, Jesse and Cynthia. Cynthia married twice, a Mr. Woodruff and a Mr. Aldrich Wells, and had issue as follows: Alilla, Polly and Betsey. Could any names be more delightful? Squire, Tubal, and Arial Manning; Abel, Jesse and Cynthia; and above all, Alilla, Polly and Betsey!

I can close my eyes this minute and see Alilla, Polly and Betsey skipping about a lawn in their muslin gowns.

. . . Unfortunately, when I close my eyes, I can also see, passing over a few generations, the family portraits of Great-grandfather Nehemiah Case and his wife, the former Sophia Jane Rowe. A couple of stern-looking characters. They were my father's grandparents and I never knew them. The only thing I know about them is that Sophia Jane had to iron the ruffles in Nehemiah's shirts twice a day before he appeared in public, and that she ironed them in silence for forty years. A patient woman. Especially since Nehemiah wasn't going anywhere in particular, except back to his leather factory.

Grandpa Case, on the other hand (my father's father), I remember vividly. His name was Francis Manning Case, as was Father's until he shortened it to Frank Case, and he was tall, white-haired, distinguished-looking, and a good deal of trouble to everybody. He too was in the leather business for a while, and then in the hotel business, but presently he gave that up and he and Grandma Case paid long and frequent visits to us at the Algonquin. One summer, both dressed in spotless white, they drove all the way from Buffalo to New York in a spanking carriage drawn by a big white horse, and were faintly amazed when it got their picture into the newspapers. They saw nothing unusual about it.

Grandpa Case used to take my little brother out for an afternoon and bring him home so stuffed with ice cream, popcorn and lollipops that a doctor had to be called in the night. Restrained from my brother, Grandpa spent his time sitting in the Algonquin lobby, humming a tuneless air and keeping time to it by drumming his fingers on the arm of his chair. This drove the people near him crazy.

"Pop," said Father one day in desperation, "how would you like it if I bought you a little inn somewhere upstate that you could run? Just something to keep you amused, you know, give you a little work to do."

Grandpa Case stopped his humming and drumming for a moment. "Work?" he said. "Look here, my boy. *I* don't care if I never do another lick of work as long as I *live!*"

As far as I know, he never did.

Grandma Case, Father's mother, was born Anna Hinson, and if you want to know about the Hinsons just go to Buffalo and ask the man in the street. If he is a traffic cop over seventy years old, he will recall the day Great-aunt Sarah Hinson tied up traffic on Richmond Avenue longer than he likes to remember.

Auntie Hinson (Grandma Case's sister) was a teacher in Buffalo's Public School Number 31 for fifty years, until she was forcibly retired with a pension when she was over seventy. The school board gave her a banquet attended by the Mayor of Buffalo and other notables who had been her pupils, and she was escorted home by a committee of them to enjoy a well-earned rest.

The only trouble was that Auntie Hinson did not enjoy resting. She was out at eight o'clock every morning, touring the town, talking to people, reporting slum conditions to her old pupil, the Mayor . . . and Auntie Hinson was not a woman who could easily be ignored. She was six feet tall, erect and handsome. She wore a black taffeta bonnet on her white hair, with black ribbons tied under her chin, and long black taffeta dresses that swept the ground. The grace of her walking was a constant source of admiration to my father, whenever she came to visit us. "She moves like a ship," he used to say.

When Auntie Hinson started walking anywhere nothing stopped her, and that was her downfall. She was accustomed to crossing Richmond Avenue at the corner nearest her house. She carried a cane in her later years, and when the city installed a traffic light at the corner of Richmond Avenue and her street, she simply flourished the cane and stopped traffic until she had crossed the street, regardless of lights. She got away with it for years.

No, she wasn't killed, or even hit by a car. She was hurt much worse—in her dignity. A Buffalo newspaper took her picture and published it over the caption: JAY-WALKER. Auntie Hinson never went out much after that.

A lifelong spinster, she lived with her bachelor brother, Great-uncle Charles Hinson, until his death some years before her own. Uncle Charlie was a judge, and had long since promised to bequeath his "library" to his nephew, Frank, my father, who was known to be a bookworm. Father's family had not much to bequeath in the way of worldly possessions, and for many years Uncle Charlie's library loomed pleasantly as a solid inheritance. I well remember the summer day it arrived at Sag Harbor. The big crate was deposited on the croquet lawn, and Father excitedly ripped off the top with a hammer and tumbled the books out onto the grass.

Uncle Charlie's library consisted of "The Public Papers of George Clinton" (whoever *he* was) in twenty volumes.

Last summer, when I was driving up to Buffalo with my son and my daughter-in-law, Sheila, to visit the relatives, I asked Sheila if she had any preconceived picture of her new relations whom she was about to meet for the first time.

"Why, sure I have," said Sheila, and lapsed into a contented silence.

"Well, tell, TELL!" my son and I shouted.

"Okay," said Sheila thoughtfully. "I think, Maggie, your cousin Flossie Young is slim, young-looking, and likes to laugh. I think she is the kind of person who . . . well, who takes your hand in both of hers and is glad to see you."

"Right!" we said.

"I think Uncle Ned Case, being your father's brother, must look like your father, only not precisely. I mean, he's not as precise-looking as your father."

"Right!" we said.

"I'm not sure about Aunt Dot. She's your father's sister so she must look something like him, but I've only seen pictures of your father, of course. I think," said Sheila, "that Aunt Dot is thin and rather snooty-looking but very humorous underneath."

"Right!" we said. "Now, what about Aunt Pansy?"

"Oh, Aunt Pansy is a cinch," said Sheila. "With that name she couldn't be anything but tiny, and frail, and somehow *clinging*. And she wears lavender perfume and a little bonnet with violets on it."

"Hoo-HAAA!" my son and I yelled hysterically. "Wait till you see Pans!"

Pans, like Auntie Hinson, is six feet tall, erect, and just about as frail and clinging as the Empire State Building. She was christened Isabel and got the name of Pansy when her father (my grandfather) picked her up out of her cradle one day and, quoting a popular song of the period, said, "You are my little pansy-blossom." How careful we must be, in speaking to our young!

Aunt Pansy (who is Mrs. Charles Underwood) is known far and wide as Pans, and will not accept her proper name of Isabel. "If I have to call up somebody and say 'This is Izz-a-bell UNN-derwood,' I feel as though I were announcing an alarm of some kind," she explains.

To my daughter-in-law, who confessed her misconception, Pans was plainly grateful. "You had the picture of me that I've always had of myself and never managed to achieve," she told Sheila. "I've always been too independent. If I had it to do over again," Pans added wistfully, "BOY! How I would CLING!"

In spite of my enjoyment of the family annals, I never filled out the application form for the Daughters of the American Revolution. For one thing, it arrived at a time when the D.A.R. were making a fuss about not allowing Marian Anderson to sing in some concert hall in Washington because she was a Negro; and both Father and I took a dim view of these proceedings.

Marian Anderson lived for many years at the Algonquin. Invariably, when she came home from a concert or whatever other distinguished appearance, she went straight upstairs in the elevator and had her meals in her room. This distressed Father, and he asked her several times to have lunch with him in the Rose Room, then the gathering-place for all the celebrities in town. When his invitations were politely declined, he had Bud telephone her and ask her to dinner with the family in the Oak Room, the popular place for dinner. Again Miss Anderson declined, but this time she wondered if Mr. Case could come to see her in her apartment for a moment.

"I know how you feel and I appreciate it," she told Father, "but there are many other people in your dining rooms and they may not all feel as you do. I would not like to take the risk of embarrassing you or myself. But thank you for your invitation, Mr. Case."

Father didn't eat a morsel of his dinner that night. And I have never felt inclined to join the D.A.R.

Father did not join the Sons of the American Revolution either, until my own son was ten years old in 1937; and then only because of a remarkable piece of foresightedness on his part. One evening he called me over to a desk in the Algonquin lobby and said, "I'm filling out these forms for The S.A.R. because, the way things are going in our blessed land, the day may come when your son has to explain *who* he *is*."

The Algonquin lobby, always unpretentious even at the height of its fame, had a small, warm, jewel-like quality —an affair of lamplight and deep colors. Its one passenger elevator generally had four or five people waiting for it, and they were often such a mixed bag as H. L. Mencken,

Fannie Brice, Marilyn Miller and Commander Evangeline Booth of the Salvation Army. Waiting for the Algonquin elevator was a special occupation, like skin-diving or being tattooed; you had to have been *through* it before you could develop any aptitude, indulgence, or affection for it. But its veterans carried a kind of accolade.

One out-of-work actor, asked by a producer if he had been unemployed during the entire season, replied, "Not exactly. I figure I put in about eight weeks waiting for the Algonquin elevator." He was hired at once.

And H. L. Mencken, approached in the lobby by an interviewer who wanted to know how he got all his ideas for books, jerked a jovial finger toward the lift and said, "You forget that I belong to the company of deep thinkers who daily congregate and wait for the Algonquin elevator. The Algonquin elevator is the *muezzin* of Forty-fourth Street. Like the Mohammedan, it climbs to its tower and makes strange noises and we below can only wait and pray. When it comes down again we go about our business as usual. There is," Mr. Mencken concluded, "plenty of time for contemplation in between."

Through the serenity of the lobby and its adjacent dining rooms, Father moved, relaxed and debonair. "Who *is* that guy?" inquired Alexander Clark, a young actor, on his first visit to the hotel. "He walks around here as though he *owned* the place!"

Father cherished the peaceful charm of his public rooms and was at pains to preserve it. Curiously, its greatest threat arose, not from any guest, but from one of the hotel's oldest and most loyal employees, Alfred Mitchell, the desk clerk. Mr. Mitchell had a clarion voice and an unfortunate phrase he was in the habit of using when an arriving guest asked for accommodations.

"WHY, YES, I GUESS I CAN FIX YOU UP!" Mitch would roar cordially.

Through years of anguished struggle against this phrase, and Mitch's booming voice, Father had developed an acute sense of hearing for both. He could hear Mitch two rooms away, and would instantly bound to the front desk and quietly plead, "Please, Mitch, *don't* say 'I can fix you up.' Say 'I think we have what you want,' or just say, 'Certainly, sir,' and give the guest the ledger to sign. And for heaven's sake, lower your voice!" Father begged. It was no use. For the more than forty years that he worked as desk clerk at the Algonk, until his death, Mitch continued to fix people up in the tones of an affectionate foghorn. He came to know all the regular patrons, of course, and took such an interest in the financial welfare of some of the younger actors and actresses that he occasionally imperilled their comfort.

"When I was just beginning as an actress," Mercedes McCambridge recalls, "I naturally wanted to live at the Algonquin, and Mitch let me have the cheapest room in the house, a tiny cell looking out on a court. I christened it the Iron Lung. Later, when I'd been in a couple of plays and had a Hollywood contract, I came back to the Algonk prepared to enjoy the luxury of a suite. But would Mitch give me one? Not on your life. 'You save your money,' he told me, 'I've got your old room for you.' And back I went into the Iron Lung."

Lovilla Veronica Bush, telephone operator at the Algonk for forty years, was another friendly soul. Stars gave "Bushie" tickets to their opening nights and seriously asked her opinion of their performances afterward. She became so well known eventually that *Cosmopolitan* magazine published a piece about her. Bushie was on the plump side, and with good Algonquin food grew so steadily plumper that she found it a tight squeeze to fit herself in between the switchboard and the counter of the front desk. When Father noticed that she was looking a little breathless, he had the switchboard moved back ten inches, at a cost of $350.

An earlier telephone operator, Florence Coles, was, innocently, my introduction to a brief life of crime. I used to get her to do my arithmetic homework for me, and then I would copy out the solutions and present them confidently at school next day. There was a rumpus when Father finally found out about that. Not only was it dishonest, he rebuked me, but did I think it was any fun for Miss Coles, with all her own work to do, to sit working out arithmetic problems? "Well, but it's no fun for me either!" I. wailed.

All of the employees seemed just like a part of my own family. Harvey, the doorman, brought a pair of rollerskates to work sometimes, and on dull days we would skate together up and down Forty-fourth Street. Harris, the bellboy, took me to school when our nurse was busy with my brother Carroll. Georges, the headwaiter, told me stories about Greek mythology to enliven my bouts with Ancient History. Georges, now retired, still comes to see me once in a while; and so many of the old crew are still at the Algonk that my every entrance there nowadays is something of a social occasion. Arthur, Philip, Earl, Al and Mike, the bellboys; August, the waiter, Raoul, the maître d'hôtel, John Martin, the manager, Nick, the room waiter, Martin, the valet, and Brownie, the porter . . . they all gather round to shake hands and gossip and reminisce about Father. Nearly all of them still call me "Miss Case" except Nick, the room waiter. Nick calls me "da Margaret."

One day last spring, Alex Clark, his wife, Frances, and I were having cocktails in the lounge when Alex excused himself for a few moments, returning to tell me that John, the attendant in the men's room had sent me his warm regards. "He says he remembers you when you were a little girl," Alex added.

"Why, of course," I said, only slightly taken aback, "I used to play in the men's room by the hour."

But on the way out I asked Alex to fetch him forth, and sure enough, we *were* old friends.

The retainers in our immediate family while I was growing up, and for many years after I was grown, were Sarah Victor, a regal-looking Negress who was pastry cook at the Algonk in the winters and our family cook at Sag Harbor in the summers, and Germaine, who was supposed to be Bud's French maid but who developed such an attachment for Father that she firmly valeted him as well. It took these two women, plus Bud, about an hour to get Father out of bed in the mornings. Although full of bonhomie once he was on his feet, he hated to get up more than anyone I ever knew. First came Germaine, who pulled up the blinds, wished him good morning, laid out his clothes for the day, and drew his bath. Then came Bud, saying "Frankie! Do you want to sleep your whole *life* away?" Then Germaine again, mourning, "Oh, but Meestair Cayze, your bot' eez getting col'!" Oddly, the most successful was Sarah, who never raised her voice above a murmur. Tiptoeing in, in her white uniform and headkerchief, she would whisper, "Boss?" with the same effect on Father as though she had run an electric charge through him.

"I'm up, I'm *up*, I'm UP!" he would shout, flinging aside the covers and reeling into the bathroom.

Once bathed and shaved, he became his sunny self again throughout the breakfast routine, which never varied. Germaine knew all the signals, so that Nick, the room waiter, would be wheeling in the breakfast table just as Father, dressed except for his coat and wearing a smoking jacket or dressing gown, appeared in the doorway between his bedroom and the living room. The following exchange then ensued, rain or shine:

Nick: Gooda morn', Mist' Case. 'Snice day today.
Father: Good morning, Nick. What did you say?
Nick: I say, 'snice day today.

I once asked Father why he made Nick repeat it. "I like to hear him say it," he explained fondly. "Just think, Nick has been in this country thirty years, and the only English sentence he has learned is a happy one."

Usually, if he was feeling particularly good, Father did a little dance step in the doorway before sitting down at the table. Breakfast was always orange juice, two three-minute boiled eggs, coffee, toast, and marmalade, but Father's way of dealing with it made it the most appetizing-looking food I have ever seen. He buttered a slice of toast on his plate, broke the eggs onto it, and then cut the whole thing meticulously into small squares. Each square of egg-on-toast on the fork was topped by a dab of marmalade just before he ate it. Somebody once shocked him by asking why he didn't order poached eggs and be done with it, if he liked eggs on toast. Father found it impossible to explain that it would not be the same thing at all.

After breakfast, while I (if it was not a schoolday)

drifted into Bud's sitting room where she was forever busy on the telephone about new linens for the hotel, or the redecorating of various suites, Father sat down in his armchair and read the *World*—or, after the *World* expired, the *Tribune*—for half an hour or so, before going down to his office on the second floor. As he grew older and his friends began to die off (as must happen to all of us who survive) Bud began to practice a thoughtful little deceit on him: every morning she carefully clipped the obituary page from the newspaper before he got it. It was a charming game they played with each other. Bud never let him know that she had removed the page, and he never let her know that he noticed it was missing.

Father's main place of business was, of course, the Algonquin dining room at lunchtime or at dinner. It was there that, visiting from table to table, he set the atmosphere of the whole place which was so largely responsible for its success. He was naturally obliged to do a good deal of work behind the scenes: ordering, comparing prices, and seeing that the hotel operated smoothly from boiler room to carpenter shop; but he could never really work himself up over the price of parsley or a leaky pipe and he was relieved when, with increasing prosperity, he was able to turn more and more of the details over to his manager and his steward, and concentrate his own attention on people instead.

He rarely left the Algonk on weekdays except for a short walk, or to go to the theatre, but Sundays were dull, and on Sundays in winter we often went out to Tarrytown, to see Elsie Janis and her mother. Elsie and Mrs. Janis lived at Philipse Manor, in an old Colonial house they had bought, with a long, wide stream and a pond where they gave fine Sunday skating parties. Douglas and

Beth Fairbanks were usually there, and Father and Bud, Irving Berlin, Billy Reardon, Forrest March, Ina Claire, Elsie Ferguson, sometimes Mary Pickford and her husband Owen Moore, and many other lively souls. I can still hear the sound of our voices and laughter falling on the air with that peculiar clarity of voices outdoors in wintertime, as we trooped back through the smoky dusk to the firelit living room for tea.

This room Mrs. Janis, with characteristic independence of spirit, had furnished with all the well-worn leather sofas and easy chairs brought from her old home in Columbus, Ohio; and while the décor was perhaps inappropriate to the pre-Revolutionary mansion where George Washington was said to have courted Mary Philipse, the room could have contained park benches alone without losing any of its conviviality and warmth. Most of its charm came from Elsie herself. She would stand with a foot on the fender, one hand shaking back her long-bobbed brown hair while the other punctuated a crackling exchange of talk. Elsie had an electric personality, and although she sought attention less than some other actresses I have known, she was the focal point of any room she entered.

Father had known Elsie and her mother since they came to stay at the Algonquin in 1906, when Elsie, aged sixteen, was starring in *The Vanderbilt Cup*. I came to know them later, during the wonderful days of *The Slim Princess*, *The Lady of the Slipper* and *The Century Girl*, and Elsie, on and off stage, grew to be the nearest thing to an idol that was possible to a child conditioned, as I was, to remain calm in the presence of celebrities. Since she could swim and ice skate like an angel I hastened to improve myself in those departments, insufferably showing off before her whenever I had the chance, with some underwater antic or outside edge. She loved the color lavender and jasmine perfume and I tried to follow her there, too, but was restrained by Father, who considered lavender and jasmine a bit too rich for my years. She could also perform almost any acrobatic feat that Douglas Fairbanks could do, and here I was brought up short by my own sheer inability. Try as I would, I was not the acrobatic type.

Because of their friendship with Father, Mrs. Janis and Elsie were very nice about having me around, and I spent many happy afternoons after school in Elsie's dressing room at the theatre. I would watch the show from the wings and, between acts, patter blissfully back to the dressing room where Hallie, Elsie's maid, would shoo me into a corner while she got Elsie ready for the next scene. Throughout the nineteen-twenties and the early 'thirties, Elsie often headlined at the Palace, with me in attendance, and it was there that I developed my abiding love for vaudeville, which lasted longer than vaudeville did. Seated out front with a pass, I rapturously watched Van and Schenck, Savoy and Brennan, Smith and Dale, Frank Fay (a single) with his courteous analysis of the lyrics of *Tea for Two*, and Lou Holtz (also a single act) with his sincere account of Archbishop Shapiro—or, as Lou Holtz used to call him, "Artsbissip Sapiro." I am told that Lou Holtz was ordered by certain authorities, not too long ago, to drop Archbishop Shapiro from his routine, on the ground that the character might offend Catholics and Jews. I can only say that I am thankful to have grown up in a tolerant age, when Catholics, Jews, and us Episcopalians lived together and talked and laughed together in the Algonquin, without fear.

At the age of fifteen I fell in love with Joe Schenck, of

the vaudeville team of Van and Schenck. Joe Schenck was small and frail, with light hair slicked back, and he sang in a falsetto tenor and played the piano rather badly. I never met him, but I prayed each night that I might. "Oh Lord," I would beseech, kneeling at my bed, "let me meet Joe Schenck." This went on until, when it seemed obvious that the Lord was not going to answer my prayer about Joe Schenck. I fell in love with a movie actor named Percy Marmont. He too was frail, slick-haired, delicate and unobtainable, since he was in Hollywood. I prayed about him exhaustively, and without success; I never got to meet him. I remember behaving quite badly about it one night when I came down to the family table for dinner, hoping against hope that I would find Joe Schenck or Percy Marmont there, and finding only Jack Barrymore.

Actually I was merely rather silent, but Mr. Barrymore was a perceptive man, and after dinner he took me out to the curb while he was getting a taxi.

"You're in love, aren't you?" he said.

"Yes," I said.

"I knew it!" said Mr. Barrymore. "That lovely, lost look, that exquisite, forlorn look; that roseleaf cheek that is not quite a blush; that brightness in the eyes that is not yet a tear. . . . Tell me, who is the man?"

"Percy Marmont," I confessed.

"*Percy Marmont!*" Mr. Barrymore cried. "That *ham?*"

The taxi drew up and Mr. Barrymore pulled me into it. "We will talk this over," he said to me, and to the driver, "Tottenham Court Road, Thibet."

We drove once around Central Park, and Mr. Barrymore urged me so strongly to forget my infatuation that I didn't have the heart to tell him I had never met Percy Marmont.

Father's friends, mostly theatre people, were always fiercely protective about me. Once, when I was in Elsie Janis's dressing room at the Palace, Father Duffy, the famous fighting chaplain of World War I, dropped in and told a mildly dirty story. I didn't get it at the time and will never know what it was, but I clearly remember Elsie, who was brushing her hair, slamming the hairbrush down on the make-up table, turning on the revered priest, and saying, "How *dare* you tell a story like that in front of a child?" I guess my own father knew the truth—that actors and actresses, if they are the right ones, are the safest friends in the world for children.

The dancing parties continued, now at the Sixty Club, and I must have driven my stepmother Bud mad, hanging around and watching her dress to go to them. Dancing dresses were lovely then—all long, floating panels of pastel-colored chiffons, caught in at the natural waistline in the manner of Irene Castle. Saddening to think that in a few short years, when I began going out to dances myself, the waistline would be around the hips and the skirts up above the knees. Father and Bud were extremely good dancers, and once even won a silver cup which, I regret to say, Bud later used as a receptacle for torn-up bits of clean newspaper for the pan of her Persian cat. One night (so Bud told me) they went out to a supper club with a party which included Irene Castle, still at the height of her fame and grace. Mrs. Castle seemed disinclined to dance with any of the men in the party, but for some reason accepted Father's invitation. As they got a quarter of the way around the floor she looked at him in astonishment and said, "Why, *you* can dance!" She then confided to him that she was obliged to be wary about the men she danced with in public because many of them were such lousy dancers that they made her look awkward on the floor, and this was bad for her professional reputation.

When Father took me to my first dancing parties at Gardner School, he faced even sterner critics among my classmates, and came through so triumphantly that I actually worked up a nice little trade in hair ribbons, vicarious homework and other favors in return for specified dances with Pa. At home, he and I used to tap around to the phonograph so constantly that he finally engaged a tap-teacher named Roy Randolph to give us lessons, and bought us each a pair of professional dancing shoes with taps. Roy Randolph insisted that we first learn a good foundation in the waltz clog. For a while it was fun, until we got so good that we could do the whole "Rosie O'Grady" routine as a team, complete with little hats with feathers. Then Father and I, mad with rhythm, wearied of the waltz clog. We wished, we announced, to go further and make like Fred Astaire. Either Mr. Randolph thought we were not ready, or perhaps we were *not* ready. At any rate, for some reason or other, the tap lessons languished . . . but our interest in dancing, never. Put on a record or whistle a tune, and we were off—together or separately.

"Like a couple of waltzing mice," Bud once remarked with a shake of the head.

* Chapter 3 *

ATHER carried his love of dancing into the home and was always hoofing lightly around the floor of the family apartment at the Algonquin, or around the living room at Sag Harbor where we lived in the summers. One day at Sag, when I was banging out *Pretty Baby* (a new tune that year) on the old salt-weathered upright, he and Douglas Fairbanks came up from the beach and promptly went into a slow foxtrot together, Father leading and Douglas following as prettily as any debutante. All the rest of that summer, Douglas called Father "Pretty Baby." "Pretty Baby want to go catch little fishies?" he would inquire tenderly if the morning promised good fishing weather.

Mr. Fairbanks was a big part of our lives at Sag Harbor from about 1913, when Father bought the place, until the 'twenties when he married Mary Pickford and went to live in California. He came down after that too, sometimes with Mary, but naturally it was not like the old days when he was a regular boarder. And I do mean boarder. He and I used to have Sunday-morning contests to see who could eat the most pancakes at breakfast. The pancakes our cook,

Sarah Victor, made were little and light and could be consumed almost indefinitely. I remember that, one Sunday, I ate nineteen and he ate twenty-seven.

Sag Harbor saw Douglas no more after his divorce from Mary and his marriage to Lady Ashley who, I guess, was not exactly the type for Sag's simple pleasures. Doug's delight in them in the early days was such, however, that Father once had to speak to him about it. We all went around the house and beach in bathing suits or old clothes —the men in slacks and sport shirts and the girls in middies and bloomers which, through the years, became abbreviated to halters and shorts; but there were two occasions when Father demanded that the girls wear dresses and the men put on jackets and, if not a collar and tie, an Ascot scarf of some kind—this was at the table, and when we went into the village. Douglas, on his first couple of weekends, drove into the village and also appeared at meals in the same costume which partially clothed him the rest of the time; dirty white duck pants, a T-shirt, and bare feet. Father's method of reproof was, as always, gently ironic.

"Are you sure you're quite comfortable, Doug?" he finally asked him as we sat down to dinner one night. "Or would you like to take off the T-shirt too?" It was the same method he used with us kids. He never said to us, "Take your elbows off the table," he just said, "Would you care for me to bring you a couch?"

Douglas barked his short gust of laughter, the kind of chuckle followed by an indrawn breath which Doug Junior now does identically, dashed upstairs like a guilty schoolboy, and came down again jacketed, scarved, and shod like a Christian.

"Pretty Baby," he said to Pa, "you-all is just clothes crazy."

Father and Douglas were an interesting contrast, pictorially. Father was lean, tall, deliberate, calm and humorous: Douglas was stocky and comparatively short (about five feet seven or eight), restless, fast-moving, and not always sure of a joke unless it was a practical joke. Together they were irresistible. Douglas always pretended publicly to think that Pa was an elegant do-nothing, and Father pretended to regard Doug as a happy illiterate. Their friendship, outwardly based on a mutual amused tolerance, was actually rooted in a deep mutual admiration and interest and, like all such firm attachments, thrived in an atmosphere of lighthearted abuse.

Douglas always had some lively project on hand when he was at Sag. One time he rigged up a Slide-for-Life, consisting of a strong rope fastened at one end to a tall oak tree on the lawn, stretched taut over the sea wall, the beach, and the water, and secured to the end of the dock about three hundred feet, or the distance of one and a half city blocks, away. To ride the Slide-for-Life you climbed a ladder into the tree, grabbed a hand pulley on the rope, kicked off, and went shooting outward and downward to land with your bottom skittering along the water in a fine shower of salt spray. Everybody fought one another off that oak tree, that summer, to ride the Slide-for-Life, including Sarah the cook. Sarah weighed about two hundred and fifty pounds, and she took part of the sea wall with her and caused something of a tidal wave when she landed, but she was so game that Douglas personally escorted her to the ladder again and again, brushing aside younger and slimmer aspirants on the way. Douglas, who was not only always willing to try anything but always eager to do it better than anyone else, admired all people with the same spirit of derring-do.

Our house, facing Shelter Island Sound, was directly across from a thickly wooded and unpopulated section of Shelter Island, and the constant view of this unexplored territory was so alluring to Douglas that he set about making a voyage of discovery. The idea of getting into Father's motorboat and crossing the three miles of water that separated him from the enchanted isle was too tame, so he and Father worked most of a day on the beach building a mast and sail into my canoe. In the late afternoon they sailed away, with the rest of us down on the dock to wave them bon voyage. A light breeze had sprung up and the little craft made good time over the water, fast becoming a speck in the distance.

Twilight fell, and then dark. It got to be dinnertime and past dinnertime, with no sign of the returning explorers. At eight o'clock Bud and I got in the motorboat and went across the Sound to see what had happened.

The canoe was pulled up on Shelter Island beach, and Father and Douglas were sitting peacefully on a driftwood log, chatting.

"The wind died down and we couldn't sail back," Father explained. "But we weren't worried—we knew you'd come for us pretty soon."

"But couldn't you have paddled back?" Bud asked.

"Oh," said Father, rather sheepishly. "Well, it seems we forgot to bring the paddles."

On the way home, towing the canoe, I asked Mr. Fairbanks what he'd found out about Shelter Island. He sprang to life with his usual enthusiasm.

"Margaret, you never saw such a fascinating place!" he told me "It's absolutely *deserted!*"

Our house at Sag was at once the most active and the most peaceful place I have ever known. We used to go down every year the day after Gardner School let out in May and stay until school opened in October. Father and Bud had to go to town most weeks to see to the Algonquin, but Carroll and I never budged for more than four long, lovely months. We arrived along with the lilac, and to this day I can't smell lilac without thinking of lying on the croquet lawn near great, heavy bushes of them, and reading Swinburne and Rupert Brooke and Yeats:

> . . . and someone called me by my name:
> It had become a glimmering girl
> With apple blossoms in her hair,
> Who called me by my name and ran,
> And faded through the brightening air.

That last line still sends shivers up my back. There was another, from Shakespeare, that electrified me under the lilacs:

> When daisies pied and violets blue;
> And lady-smocks all silver-white,
> And cuckoo-buds of yellow hue
> *Do paint the meadows with delight.* . . .

The italics are mine. I know now that Mr. Shakespeare was being satirical, and so, perhaps, was Mr. Yeats. But the sheer beauty of those single lines was enough to make me, at fourteen and fifteen, forget the context even if I had understood it. I became so bookish that it made my stepmother nervous.

"Margaret!" she would exclaim, coming upon me in the act of wolfing down a book. "*Don't* read it all at once— you'll get to the end and have nothing left!"

"Oh, yes I will," I would reply absently with my head in the pages. "I can always read it over again."

This sounded idiotic to Bud, but her idea of allotting yourself one chapter at a time seemed as senseless to me as skipping dinner one day in order to enjoy it the next. Bud was a conscientious stepmother to a couple of kids who must have seemed pretty weird to her at times. I once had a favorite pink kimono girdled with a sash but with no other fastening; whenever I donned this garment, I would bend over and hold the two front hems together until they were absolutely even and then inch my way up the front, holding the edges together to make sure that the front hems were even to a hair's breadth where they met, before I put on the sash. They never came out even enough to suit me, and Bud said later that she sometimes looked on in pure incredulity while I went through this performance fifteen or twenty times.

Carroll's peculiarities were more normal, concerned with the usual childish sins such as failing to brush his teeth night and morning, but his reaction to reproof was sometimes unexpected. One time Bud, getting after him about the toothbrush matter, said, "I know you didn't brush your teeth this morning, because I just felt your toothbrush and it's bone dry."

The next morning the little six-year-old master mind sauntered into her room, ostentatiously wiping his toothbrush on a towel. "Isn't it strange, Bud," he remarked, "how few people dry their toothbrushes?"

At night, at Sag Harbor, we all usually went for the last swim of the day just before bedtime. The water, clearer and more velvety during the day than anything this side of the Mediterranean, was filled with phosphorus at night so that when you swam under water with your eyes open (and who would swim under water any other way?) great silvery balls of it flashed past you, and your path was outlined in white fire. Then, when you climbed out and lay down on the dock and looked up at the crowded stars, a curious thing happened; you felt as if you were floating up, up to the stars, as if your body were suspended in space. Years later, when I read about the Hindu's Nirvana, I imagined it must be something like the way I used to feel at night on the dock at Sag Harbor.

Bedtime swimming continued into October when the water was so cold and the air so nippy that we would quickly wrap ourselves in woolen robes and race back to the house and a big open fire, and sit around for a while talking and eating apples from the two apple trees Father had planted one year as a birthday present to me. There was never any nonsense about hot toddies, or even hot tea or chocolate; we swam in cold water, we ran through chilly night air, and we ate cold apples. I may be wrong, but I attribute to this practice the fact that I have never had a cold in my life.

Our Spartan routine was sometimes too much for house guests, and more than once I saw Joseph Hergesheimer, Carl Van Vechten, Franklin P. Adams or Robert Benchley huddled on the dock in a heavy overcoat, watching our icy water-sports with something like horror. One night, back in the house, F.P.A. wrapped his coat tighter, glared around him, and said with a shudder, "I need a drink. What do you have to *do* to get a drink around here—turn up embalmed in a glacier like the Lost Bridegroom?" He got his drink, of course. Although Father and many of his friends, including Douglas, never drank (at least Douglas didn't at that time), there was always liquor for anyone who wanted it.

An English actor named Kenneth Douglas was even more vocal concerning our October nighttime swims. "Frank," he said earnestly to Father, "I can be cold at home in England. I did not come to the land of central heating in order to freeze on a small pier at Long Island."

"Well, nobody asked you to," said Father mildly, and this was true. We never urged anyone to join us, or even to watch us. Our guests simply seemed to feel that the whole idea was so improbable that they had better appoint themselves a squad of private eyes to see whether we would go through with it.

Freezing on a small pier was not the worst thing that happened to Kenneth Douglas at Sag Harbor. He came down one weekend with another English actor named Barry Baxter, and they both expressed a desire for some real American lobster. We dug our own scallops out of our front yard, so to speak, and our clams from a nearby creek, but for live lobster we had to drive to Montauk, twenty-five miles away, and buy them from the lobstermen there. This was my duty, and I loved it. I had started driving the family station wagon, a Model-T Ford, when I was thirteen—they were not so fussy about licenses then and Harold Morouney, the motorcycle cop, was a good friend of ours—so when we wanted lobsters off I'd go tinkety-tinkety along the rocky dirt road to Montauk, singing all the way. It was a truly bad road in those days, full of twists and turns and small boulders that bounced the little Ford into the air like a bubble off a soap-bubble pipe. I drove the Ford at its full speed of forty-five miles an hour and sometimes, after a rain, it would skid in the

mud exactly in rhythm to the song I happened to be singing and I would keep it skidding that way until I finished
the song. If ever an automobile and a driver danced together, it was the Ford Model-T and me.

It was to this vehicle of potential death that Kenneth
Douglas and Barry Baxter invited themselves by saying
that they would like to drive to Montauk with me, to get
the lobsters. They wanted to see more of LONG-island, as
Englishmen always call it.

The Model-T station wagon of that period was entirely
unenclosed except for a top and a few wooden slats de-
signed to hold curtains when it rained. Riding in it, even
ordinarily, was like riding an open-air trolley car at ten
times the speed of a trolley car. Riding in it with me at
the wheel was like travelling in a chicken coop in a hurricane. It wasn't long before I heard plaintive sounds from
my passengers in the back seat, but on looking over my
shoulder I found that Mr. Douglas was still wearing his
monocle so I concluded that he was safe, and we pressed
on to Montauk and got the lobsters. They were stowed as
usual, live and protesting in baskets, on the floor of the
station wagon behind the back seat, and we started home.

Five miles along the road I will be darned if Mr. Douglas and Mr. Baxter didn't start the same old caterwauling
about slowing down. This time I paid them no heed. I
considered these gents a couple of fusspots, and my job
was to get the lobsters home to Sarah in time to cook them
for dinner. Finally, however, Mr. Douglas and Mr. Baxter
made so much noise that I pulled up to the side of the
road and stopped the car.

"What on earth is the matter?" I asked. One look told
me what was the matter.

The lobsters had escaped from the baskets and were

swarming over the two matinee idols like a bunch of teen-agers. One small one, undoubtedly female, had knocked off Mr. Douglas's eyeglass and was kissing him passionately all over his face. A big one was sitting upright on Mr. Baxter's lap and punching him in the nose. The others were climbing up their trousers, peeking over their shoulders, and peering into their ears. If ever I saw two English actors covered with lobsters, they were Mr. Douglas and Mr. Baxter.

In later years I was to admire British fortitude and British tranquillity, but Mr. Douglas and Mr. Baxter showed neither of those qualities that day. They yelled their heads off. I picked the lobsters off them and put them back in the baskets, and we went on home, lickety-split by request from the back seat. My passengers couldn't wait to get out of that man-eating car.

That night at dinner, in the very act of consuming the dear creatures who had tried to make friends with them, Mr. Douglas and Mr. Baxter told the whole story with many complaints about my driving, about the state of the Montauk road, about the vicious habits of lobsters. They were really quite upset about it, to a point where even Father grew a little weary. An eyebrow from him had already told me to keep quiet, and I was not surprised by his next remark. Father had a gift for seeming to continue a conversation when he was through with it, and his tact was always like a healing flow of cool water.

"I wonder where the word 'lobster' came from?" he said, cutting into his chop. He wasn't allowed to eat lobster on account of a nervous stomach. "Margaret, get the dictionary."

"Lobster," he read aloud, peering over his plate at the page while we all sucked our lobster claws, "from the

Latin *locusta*. Hm-m-m. Any large marine macrural crustacean used as food . . ." I could see from Father's expression that, for once, Mr. Webster had fallen down on him; a lobster was just a lobster, nothing interesting about it. However, Father did not fail Mr. Webster. He went on reading, as though from the page, and making up definitions as he went along. Nobody at the table knew what he was doing except me; I knew the nuances.

"The syllable 'lob' is from the Greek, meaning in, of, or from a certain source," Father informed us gravely, "and the termination 'ster' obviously refers to habitat, trade, or profession."

"As in 'Ham-ster,' I said uncontrollably with a glance at our English actors.

"Or like Oy-ster!" cried Carroll, making gestures like a Jewish comedian.

"Or like Spin-ster," I said, rotating an imaginary spinning wheel.

"Or like Cus-ster!" said Carroll, making like a Last Stand and starting to unleash a string of oaths until Bud shushed him.

"Or like Bus-ster," said Father peaceably, throwing Bud a kiss, or a buss.

"Or like Sis-ster," cried Caroll, giving me a Bronx cheer.

"Or like *bannister!*" cried Kenneth Douglas suddenly. A silence fell. "Bannister?" Father asked.

"Yes, certainly! As in 'I hereby bannis you from my presence.' Doesn't that make me a bannister?" said Mr. Douglas.

It made him a bannister, all right, or anything he wanted to be, with our family. We loved him from that time on.

We spent the rest of that evening playing charades, and

I stumped the company by hoofing around in a dishpan, representing a word. In-de-pan-dance, of course. Nevertheless, Father came into my room when I was getting ready for bed and looked at me seriously.

"You know, you've got to be careful driving when you have Englishmen in the car," he told me. "We're apt to forget that, only a couple of years ago, these men were lying in trenches and being shot at. Maybe their nerves aren't as strong as ours. Good night, dear," he said, and kissed me and went across the hall to his own room.

I think of that so often these days—two wars later— whenever I visit a hospital or talk to a veteran, wounded or whole. Sure, the boys love to laugh, and to be back in a country where laughter is important; but they have seen things I have no conception of. Father knew that, thirty years ago.

My stepmother, Bud, soon plucked me from my happy racketing in the Model-T Ford. She claimed, rightly, that I was too lazy to learn to drive a real car, one with a gear-shift, and she set out in her efficient way to teach me without my knowing it. We met accidentally in the village late one afternoon, me in the Model-T and Bud in her Hudson Super-Six roadster, and started to drive home at the same time—Bud passing me on the North Haven road, just across the bridge. A little farther on she put out her hand and stopped, and so, naturally, did I. Bud got out of the Hudson, walked back to the Ford, nudged me out of the driver's seat and took the wheel.

"I'll drive the Ford home," she said. "You drive the Hudson."

It was like being thrown off a dock and told to swim. Aside from one or two tentative lessons on a deserted back road, I had never driven the Hudson or any car with a gearshift. With a Model-T Ford you had three pedals—clutch, reverse, and brake—and an emergency brake; the speed was controlled by a hand throttle on the steering wheel which you pulled downward when you wanted to go faster, and which I generally kept pulled down as far as it would go. Now, as Bud disappeared in this cherished car, I was left alone in the gloaming, three and a half miles from home and faced with a monster full of fancy gears and a foot accelerator. If I wanted to get home for dinner I darn well had to drive it. So I sighed, climbed in, and lay down. It was one of those low-slung affairs you were obliged to lie down in and peer through the spokes of the steering-wheel, not over its top.

"Swing low, sweet chariot," murmured Mr. John Drew, who was standing in the doorway when I finally swept around the drive and pulled up with a grand jerk, stalling the motor. He had driven over from his own summer home in Easthampton with his niece, Ethel Barrymore. Miss Barrymore was sitting on a rock on the lawn in her familiar attitude of resting a cheek on her hand. That lady, I swear, could look more queenly sitting on a little old rock than most queens look on a throne.

If Bud ever regretted her insistence on my driving that day she never said so, but it was her last chance at the Hudson. From that time I was seldom out of it, breezing all over Long Island with (on one occasion) a special trip to Amagansett Court House to take care of a ticket presented to me for doing fifty or better on the Easthampton road where the speed limit was forty. This episode I blame entirely on Father's cigars. It was a strange state trooper who picked me up, and in my most winning way I set about bribing him. Father, over my dead body, had taken the Hudson a week or so earlier to drive to Southampton, and I knew he had a habit of putting a couple of cigars in the side pocket. I reached in, and sure enough, there they were. Sweetly, I handed one to the state trooper and it crumbled to powder and blew away on the summer wind.

"Some cigars!" I said bitterly to Father when I told him about it. I thought he would laugh himself off the bathhouse steps.

"*I* didn't put any cigars in the pocket the day I went to Southampton," he said. "Those must have been a couple of cigars from last summer!"

My brother didn't let me forget this little incident for some time. "*Do* have a cigar, nice, kind, lovely officer!" he would urge, bowing low and handing me a bunch of seaweed. Then he would push me off the dock.

The chic position for driving a roadster in those days, in addition to sitting on the middle of your spine, was to drape the right arm negligently around the steering wheel with the left arm in your lap and the fingers of the left hand turned up and barely touching the wheel from underneath. As a result of such elegance my right arm and hand were always tanned to a deep mahogany by October while the left remained lily-white. This was before dedicated sun-bathing, or the passion for acquiring an even tan. In those times you got a tan on whatever part of your body your activities happened to expose to the sun. After a summer of heavy digging for soft clams, for instance, you were likely to be a rich brown behind the knees.

I think I drove the Hudson for at least five summers. When I inherited the family's Chrysler roadster, Father gave the Hudson to Frank Corwin, a neighbor, and years later, after I was married and a mother, Mr. Corwin asked me in one day and showed me my former juggernaut, up on jacks in his barn. How my mighty monster had shrunk! The great balloon tires, enormous and powerful in my mind's eye, looked about the size of today's steering wheels.

Father let the women of his family do most of the driving, preferring to be a passenger. As a passenger, he had his eccentricities. He didn't like to see trees coming at him, for one thing. Even when the car was tooling along a straight road with the trees in their usual orderly lines at each side, Father had an idea that they were coming at him and he would dodge and duck like a cornered wild thing, never relaxing until we got to some place like Shinnecock Hills where there *were* no trees. He was happiest in a town car he bought which had a little window with a roller shade between himself in the back seat and Gourley, the chauffeur, in front. Father would roll down the blind so that he couldn't see anything ahead of him, and then he would sit back pleasurably and light a cigar. Staring at this black shade often gave Bud and me the feeling that we were rushing into an abyss, but it rested Father so we made no complaints.

Another problem, on our spring and fall treks to and from Sag Harbor, was Father's need of what he called "plenty of footroom." He had long legs and he liked to be able to move his legs and feet around without any hampering objects in the way. This was a puzzlement, since you don't move a whole family one hundred and twenty-five miles to the country or home again without certain impedimenta creeping into the car. In our case they consisted of, in the spring:

Bud's Persian cat in basket
Sarah's canary, John MacCormack, in cage

Potted plants from Algonquin lobby and family's
apartment to be transplanted in garden

Assortment of books and/or toys from which Carroll
and I would not be separated at last minute

Small rug, several vases, or other *objets d'art* which
Bud thought would look well at Sag

And, coming back in the fall:

Cat in basket

Canary in cage

Potted plants from garden to be installed in Algonquin
lobby and family's apartment

Different assortment of books and/or toys from which
Carroll and I would not be separated at last minute

Six dozen jars of jam, jelly, pickles, preserves, put up
by Sarah during summer

Three shoe boxes of horsechestnuts gathered by me
and destined to rot under bed all winter

In the spring, Gourley and Germaine would stow these
things on the floor of the car about half an hour before we
were due to take off, being careful to leave an island of
space for Father's feet and legs. (Sarah had gone down by
train a day or so earlier to open the house.) Then Germaine and Gourley would sit up front and Bud, Carroll,
and I would arrange ourselves in back, taking up as little
room as possible. Presently, debonair as a spring breeze,
came Father. He was always last, partly because he liked
to wait until the fuss was over and partly because so many
people stopped him on his way out of the hotel that it
always took him ten or fifteen minutes to get out of the
front door. Sometimes, if it got to be really late, he would
go around through the kitchen and out the back door.

Vasiliu

"Well! Are we ready?" Father would ask, strolling up to the packed and vibrating car and adjusting his country hat, a dark green Alpine number with a little feather in the band.

"No," Bud would say, "I have to go back and do a week's washing."

"No," I would say, "I have to go back and do my homework."

These were stock answers and Father lightly ignored them. There was one response he could not overlook, however.

"I have to go to the bathroom," Carroll usually said.

Waiting for Carroll's return, Father would get into the space reserved for him and his feet and legs and politely endeavor to fit them into it. It was always a failure. Potted plants, canaries, and cats went flying every time he stretched and this distressed Father, who would not purposely have harmed any living thing. He finally solved the dilemma by buying a Buick station wagon and sending Gourley ahead with Sarah and the plants, pets, and other "polyphenalia," as Sarah used to call it; then Gourley would come back by train and drive us down, a couple of days later, in the gloriously empty car.

It took Father a whole year to adjust himself to the luxury of all this unaccustomed space. The first time he saw the uncluttered floor of the car, with all the room in the world for his legs and feet, he gazed around it in dismay and his eyebrows shot up under the brim of his Alpine skimmer.

"Where *is* everything?" he wanted to know.

Whether he was going to Sag Harbor, California, or Europe, Father had the gift of travelling empty-handed. His method of departure was to put on his hat, coat and gloves and walk out of the front door without a backward glance. Nor, except in the semi-annual trek to and from Sag Harbor, did his wife or children have to carry anything either. We all drifted off light as air and somehow, when we got to our cabins on the ship or compartments in the train or eventual foreign hotel rooms, the luggage was always there waiting, and magically unpacked. Father had the same way of leaving foreign hotels, trains and ships, and to see him breeze through Customs was a pleasure. In all the years I travelled with him, I don't remember seeing a Customs inspector open one trunk or valise.

Much of this relaxed manner must, of course, be credited to Germaine who looked after the details, and even more to Bud, whose talent for organization always kept things running smoothly. Bud never fussed; she never had to, for she always planned the minutiae of living in advance and she expected other people to co-operate. At Sag, for instance, nobody, family or guest, was late to meals. If you were going to be unavoidably detained somewhere and you let her know in time, lunch or dinner would be kept and served to you when you wanted it; but there was no accidental straggling in to the table after the specified hour. Not that Bud ever said anything; again she didn't have to; she was capable, on such an occasion, of silently icing the atmosphere for a good twenty feet around her.

At bedtime at Sag, Bud would half-jokingly assign a certain chore to each member of the party, guest or family, to be done on the following day; painting the garden furniture, weeding the delphinium bed, and so on. It was no joke, we found out, if we forgot or neglected it. Bud was no martinet, far from it; but she herself was constantly busy with something constructive or other, and she liked to see people busy around her. She disliked anyone who was lazy or shiftless in his habits, or with his life, and her strongest criticism was to say of someone, "He doesn't pull his weight in the boat."

Although we may have done some groaning over our labors at the time I think, looking back, that all of that planned activity accounted for much of the happiness and serenity at Sag. And there was always plenty of time for loafing, too. I usually did most of mine on the deck of Father's boat while the others were fishing in the cockpit, and Bud did not complain of this, although she failed to understand it. She could never see how I could lie up there in the sun doing nothing when the glorious excitement of dragging a fish from the salty depth was mine for the asking. Bud was a poor sailor and did not care much for boats, but she was an intense and dedicated fisherman and would squeal her head off if she boated a two-pound porgy. She got almost the same pleasure out of growing flowers and shrubs that she did out of killing fish, and the gardens at Sag Harbor, under her care (and that of the squads of gardeners, professional and otherwise, which she recruited), grew to be so beautiful and luxuriant that they supplied not only all the flowers for the house and neighbors, but for the Algonquin as well. One of Bud's greatest joys was weeding after a rain when the weeds come out, root and all, with a kind of reluctant *"plop!"* "I like the sound they make," she said once. But, even though she loved to weed, she would never let a bush or a tree be pruned, or even a dying one be cut down. When either of these measures became absolutely necessary, Father had to wait until a day when Bud happened to be in New York, and sneak the operation in during her absence. She was a cool blonde who never wept that I recall, but Germaine remembers her crying like a child, one time, over a tree that had been felled.

Vegetables, too, flourished in the Sag Harbor garden, and Bud naturally came up with the practical idea of making the whole thing a paying proposition. Although our summer home was never known to any of us except as Sag Harbor or Sag, Father had, in some dim past, christened it Shore Acres after a long-ago play by James A. Herne. Father could have had little acquaintance with James A. Herne, who died in 1901, although he did know his daughter, Chrystal Herne, who was the original Craig's Wife in George Kelly's play of that name. Perhaps he named the place Shore Acres because Robert Edeson, a neighbor at Sag, once played in Shore Acres. . . . No, Robert Edeson didn't. I just looked it up in Daniel Blum's Theatre Book. Well, then *why?*

Here ensues one of those brief periods of research dear to the heart of the writer because it involves great thumbing of reference books, much telephoning to authorities, and no typing whatever.

"Webster's Biographical Dictionary" gives James A. Herne and his plays, including one called *Sag Harbor*. Is this a clue? No, because we already *called* the place Sag Harbor, and if Father wanted to name the place after a play by James A. Herne why would he pick one called *Shore Acres?*

"Webster's Biographical Dictionary" does not mention Robert Edeson.

Daniel Blum's "A Pictorial History of the American Theatre"—which, may I courteously murmur, has the quaintest index I ever saw—gives eleven references to

Robert Edeson, two to James A. Herne, none whatever to *Shore Acres*.

George Freedley of the Theatre Department at the New York Public Library, when called on the phone just now, says that *Shore Acres* was produced on Broadway, without Robert Edeson, in 1893.

"Eighteen-ninety-*three!*" I shrieked. "Impossible! Father hadn't even come to *New York* then!"

Mr. Freedley, a good friend of Father's, rebuked me gently. "There *were* plays on Broadway," he pointed out, "before Frank Case came to New York."

"I suppose so," I said doubtfully. Meantime Mr. Freedley had been dipping into the files again.

"Robert Edeson," he said, "was in *Shore Acres* in Boston."

"Road company?"

"Road company."

"Then he wouldn't have talked about it much. I still can't figure out why Father named the Sag Harbor place Shore Acres. Well, it doesn't matter much, since everybody forgot the name immediately anyway. But thank you very much, Mr. Freedley."

This last came from the heart, for:

> Who could write a book indeedly,
> Without the aid of old George Freedley?

End of brief period of research.

At any rate, Bud resurrected the name Shore Acres for the paying farm she had in mind, and promptly had a thousand handsome billheads printed bearing the legend:

Shore Acres Farm, Sag Harbor, Long Island, Box 893. Father, the purist, objected to the wording.

"You can't call a place Shore Acres Farm," he ruled, a little too strictly perhaps. "It's redundant. The word 'farm' implies 'acres' and besides, it doesn't sound right. You might just as well say *Romeo and Juliet and Max*."

Whether for that reason or another, the paying-farm idea dwindled away, although Sag Harbor (or Shore Acres) continued to supply large amounts of vegetables and fruit to the Algonquin menu. The overhead cost was not excessive since, under Bud's prodding, not only the hired gardeners but everybody on the place helped pick, wrap, crate and ship. Sarah used the backs of the Shore Acres Farm billheads to write grocery lists on, and our summer home once more became to us just Sag Harbor, or, fondly, Sag.

Father, as I have often said, was a demon for the proper use of words; and he was a super-demon about the careless garbling of quotations. Only Franklin P. Adams, the ultra-demon purist, could match his pained look when someone said something like, "Alas, poor Yorick, I knew him well," or "Romeo, Romeo, wherefore *art* thou, Romeo?" In the second quotation the inflection was, of course, what mattered, and Father would kindly explain to clods that Juliet was not asking where Romeo was—he was right there under the balcony—but inquiring of an unkind fate why he had to mess up everything by being Romeo. Sometimes, to make his point, Father recited the line in dialect. "Alzo, for why you are Romeo, tell me?" he would say, German-Yiddish, or "What FOH is you-all Romeo?", Southern United States. He always convinced his listeners, but seldom before he and they had broken up into helpless laughter over the whole thing.

Father never laughed off a misquotation, however, until he had gotten it right. If it was one that he was not himself positive about, he waited, looked it up, and next time he saw you, sprang the correct version. One day, I remember, I said lightly apropos of something or other, "Ah, well, hanging and wiving go by destiny." Two or three days later, when I came into the Algonk for lunch, Father sat down at my table.

"It's 'hanging and wiving *goes* by destiny,' not 'go,' although don't ask me why," he said at once. I said I thought "go" sounded better, Father agreed, and we then embarked upon an impromptu verbal rewriting, vastly entertaining to us, of the English classics. I don't remember our improvements, except that we took all the "heynonny!" business out of the sixteenth century and felt better for it.

Father never sounded reproachful when he corrected you about a misquotation or a word that seemed wrongly used. He was just enormously interested, and he made you interested, too. I think he would have made a fine teacher, and sometimes when I consider my son Case Morgan and his success as an English master at Lawrenceville, his enthusiasm for his subject and his gift for communicating it to his students, I am convinced that he got it from his grandfather, Frankie.

Perhaps because Father's mind was always busy with something, he had no small talk. The weather, except for its effect on fishing and the garden, or (in the case of hurricanes) our own lives, had no place in his conversation. Neither did the state of his health, or anyone else's. Such platitudes bored him, and he quickly eeled away from anyone who offered no better talk. Frankie, himself, would as soon have killed a man as bore him, and he expected the same consideration from other people.

As a hotelkeeper, he naturally did not always get it. Not all of the residents of the Algonquin were the writers and theatre people Father loved. Many of them were old ladies who carried canes and who, armed with this third support, could outstand Father for what seemed like hours while they told him about the state of their health and the state of the weather. Father was always charming to them; as a hotel man it became him to be patient, and besides, he was naturally polite. But he was never socially helpless. I think I was about ten years old when I first learned to discover exactly when Father was in a spot, and unobtrusively to get him out of it. When the distress signal reached me—and I have forgotten what it was; Father never sent out any obvious flares—I would stroll to the bellboys' bench and send a boy with the message that Mr. Case was wanted urgently on the telephone. I then had to call him on the phone, from a booth in the lobby, because Father would not allow me to tell a lie. Generally I just said, "Father?" and he said, "Thank you, Margaret."

But children are strange. As my role of bore-detector grew, so did my imagination. One evening I called Father as usual from the phone booth, to save him from some old lady, and I said, "Father? You know my room? Well, I'm in it, and it's on fire."

I still claim I got a spanking for that, although Father always maintained that he never touched me, however tempted.

Father, in fact, could never spank his children because it gave him a stomach-ache. He was incapable of spanking a child in cold blood, and if he did it in anger, he got a pain. I think it was mostly self-preservation, and sound reasoning, that made him so even-tempered. The Cases were born irritable ("How else could we have helped to win the War of the Revolution?" my Aunt Jenny once inquired), and Father was one of the few Cases who learned to curb his natural explosiveness. Even he didn't always succeed.

I think, since I have so far presented Father as an angel (which he was), I should also give the other side of him. There was only a flash of it now and then, but like Shakespeare's little candle, its beams were piercing.

Charles Hanson Towne had a favorite story about Father trouncing some drunk who jostled him one night on the pavement outside Shanley's restaurant, but Father always denied this tale, remarking loftily that he would not soil his hands on a drunk. He himself admitted, though, that once, catching the Algonquin vegetable cook stirring milk into the mashed potatoes after repeated instructions not to do so, he picked up the cauldron of potatoes and threw it across the hotel kitchen, and then picked up the vegetable cook and threw him out the back door.

I was personally witness to only one outburst of Father's. Bud, one day, was opening a box of gardenias sent to her by Speed Gaynor, a family friend who had danced with her the night before at a party, when Father came into the room. "Who are those flowers from?" he demanded. "Speed Gaynor," said Bud. "He just thought he'd send me some flowers . . ."

She got no further. Father grabbed the gardenias and hurled them across the room, and cast the box after them. "Tell him not to do it again," he said. And he went out of the door and slammed it behind him.

It was the first time I had ever seen my father in a temper, and I was shocked. But it was also the first time I had seen a tender smile around my stepmother's mouth, and I guess it was then that I realized they loved each other.

The sunny quiet of Sag Harbor, and Bud's own talent for tranquillity were a refuge to Father from too many overchatty elderly dames at the Algonk, and he sank into it like a tired child into a feather bed. One Sunday, he and Bud and I were sitting on the lawn—Bud doing some sewing, and Pa and I working the Tribune crossword puzzle. We always got two Tribunes on Sunday so that Father and I could race each other to the finish. Suddenly I realized that Father wasn't working at his puzzle. I looked up and saw him gazing with utter contentment at Bud and me.

"What other man is as fortunate as I!" he exclaimed. "Here I am, sitting with the two women in my family, and neither one of you has spoken a word for half an hour!"

. . . We sold Sag Harbor, in 1947 after Father and Bud died. One day that summer, sitting on the dock, I decided I didn't want to live there alone.

I could picture the dock as I had known it, swarming with laughing people. Douglas Fairbanks popping over the side with a seaweed beard; William Farnum, who had a house along the beach, sailing up in his yacht and inviting everybody aboard—Mr. Farnum was then making ten thousand dollars a week in the movies and notably spending every cent; Mr. Drew, whom I never saw in a bathing suit, but who liked to sit around on the dock benches and talk, clad in his usual white flannels and panama hat; De Wolfe Hopper, who wore a wig as everyone knew, but a magical wig to me because it stayed on even when he swam backward under water; and his wife, a beautiful young woman named Elda, who is now known to millions of Hollywood gossip-readers as Hedda.

I shook myself out of this revery. "Oh come, Maggie," I told myself, "if you're going to get sentimental over Hedda Hopper you better just haul off and sell the place."

I slid off the dock and turned toward the house, and that was what decided me. I actually expected to hear the screen door open and slam (it always slammed) and to see Father, jaunty in a yachting cap, stride down the flagstone path to the beach.

"I'd get spooky if I lived here alone," I thought.

So we sold Sag Harbor.

* Chapter 4 *

WHEN, owing to a visual memory which enabled me to retain each printed page of my schoolbooks just long enough to recite it satisfactorily in class, I was graduated from Gardner School at seventeen, a year ahead of myself, Father offered me a choice of going to Vassar or going to school for a year in France and then going to Vassar. I took the entrance examination for Vassar and came out fairly well except for a large condition in mathematics.

"I guess you'd better go to France for a year," said Father sadly. "But how are we going to send you over?"

Bud, who had been quiet for a long time, spoke up. "Send her over?" she said. "Nonsense. We will take her."

So I never did get to Vassar, but spent two years in France for which I am forever grateful. As for my classical education at home, Miss Masland at Gardner, God bless her, had taught me at least enough Latin so that I am able to follow the conversations between Lord Peter Wimsey and Harriet in the detective novels of Dorothy L. Sayers. It is only when Wimsey and Harriet lapse into the original Greek that I faintly regret the loss of Vassar.

We sailed on the *Adriatic*, and I still have the bon voyage note Mr. John Drew sent me: it is scrawled on mourning paper with a deep black edge (Mrs. Drew had just died) and it came with a basket of fruit.

> Dear Margaret, (Mr. Drew wrote)
>   In case you're not violently ill during the voyage, eat some of this fruit and the activity of your illness —if you are ill at all—may be accelerated.
>   I hope you find a fine school and have a lovely and *studious* time.
>   Affectionately yours,
>   John Drew

Not a brilliant message, perhaps, but I treasure it because Mr. Drew taught me more about the English language than anybody, except possibly Father. Mr. Drew taught me how to pronounce the words "exquisite," "congratulate," "height," "miscellany," "amateur," and the simple word, "you." Sometimes, when I listen to emcees on television nowadays, I wish Mr. Drew were still alive.

Another gift that came to me on board the *Adriatic* had me in a romantic dream for a while. It was a tiny corsage, delivered fresh every morning by the steward, no card enclosed. Some prince on board, I decided, who had become dazzled by my charms. On the last day, as we nosed into Southampton, the last corsage arrived, and there was a card with this one.

"Hope you liked the flowers," it read. "Love from Elsie and I."

                              (Signed) Ma Janis

Bud had been in France during the war, when she joined the Y.M.C.A. and went over with Elsie and Mrs.

Janis. But none of us had ever been to England, so we were going to stop over in London for a week or two before going on to Paris. If I had one experience of my life to live over, I think I would choose my first sight of London, when I was seventeen. I have lived in France, and I love it. I love Paris in the springtime, I love Paris in the fall. But for pure, stunning majesty, for a city that draws you into itself until you become a part of it, and are helplessly in love with it, give me London before World War II.

I left Father and Bud in the hotel and, armed with a map, immediately started exploring all the exciting places: Fleet Street, Baker Street, Lincoln's Inn Fields, Wapping Old Stairs, High Holborn, Tottenham Court Road. . . . I covered most of them in a day, mainly by walking, partly by leaping onto any passing bus that bore an attractive name.

Tired and happy, I returned to the hotel about six o'clock, and found Edmund Goulding there, having tea with Father and Bud. I do not complain, but it is a fact that you could not visit any city in the United States or Europe without running into friends of Father's.

"I say!" said Eddie to Father, "I saw this daughter of yours walking down a rather unsavory street today, entirely alone, with her nose in a guidebook sort of thing. Do you think that's quite—er—*quite?*"

"Quite," said Father.

Even Father's forbearance tottered, however, when I informed him that I wished to forget this nonsense about going to school in Paris and would prefer instead to take lodgings in Bloomsbury and write stories for *Pearson's* and *The Strand Magazine*. "I won't need any money," I told him sublimely. "I've read every story in all the English magazines since we came here, and I can write them too. And just think," I went on, all of a glow, "I can eat *every day* at the Cheshire Cheese!"

Father might reasonably have pointed out that I couldn't sign checks at the Cheshire Cheese as I was accustomed to do at the Algonquin (or at the Carlton, where we were staying), but he said nothing, merely regarding me with his own form of exasperation—the cocked eyebrow.

"Thomas Chatterton," I went on feverishly, rushing headlong to destruction, "lived and died in Bloomsbury when he was only nineteen, and look what *he* wrote!"

Father chose a cigar from his humidor, clipped the end with his gold cutter, lit up, and eyed me with flattering interest.

"*What* did Thomas Chatterton write?" he asked.

He had me there.

"I don't know, either," said Father. He picked up the telephone and made our reservations for France for the following week. On his way out of the room to dress for dinner, he gave me a little pat on the shoulder. "Don't feel bad about Bloomsbury," he said. "Thomas Chatterton lived and died in Holborn."

I looked up Thomas Chatterton in a book the next day and, do you know, Father was right.

He was as much addicted to the Johnsonian atmosphere of the Cheshire Cheese as I, however, and had been so ever since the day Percy Waxman, then editor of *Pictorial Review*, took us there to sample a special, surprise dish. It looked like individual meat pies and we ate ours heartily, only a little mystified by the needlelike bones we encountered.

"Fish?" Father asked Percy. "It doesn't taste like fish, but these bones. . . ."

"Not fish," said Percy. Not until our plates were clean would he tell us what it was.

"It's lark-and-kidney pie!" he then announced triumphantly.

Father turned paler than a suet pudding.

"Lark?" he whispered. "Do you mean that *I* . . . have *eaten* . . . a *lark?*"

"Oh, probably two or three," Percy informed him jovially. "They're tiny beggars, y'know; takes several to make one good pie."

I was no help to Father. I looked at the forlorn, stripped little bones and in my literary way sorrowfully quoted—or rather, misquoted:

> *"Hark! Hark! The lark!*
> *"And Phoebus 'gins arise. . . ."*

"Be *quiet*, MARGARET!" Father shouted on a rising scale. "Phoebus," he explained, visibly controlling himself, "is not the only thing that 'gins arise."

We later knew Percy Waxman and his wife, Connie, as two of the merriest, kindest people in the world. They became, not only good friends of the Algonk, but frequent and welcome guests at the family's summer home in Sag Harbor. I am quite sure that it was Connie Waxman who once wanted Percy to buy her a racehorse because she had thought of such a perfect name for one: "Slow but Sure."

We were, as I said, always running into friends of Father's and Bud's. One afternoon, at the Carlton, Father called into my room, "Come out and say hello to Miss de Forest." Miss Marian de Forest, an intellectual lady in tweeds, was a sometime playwright and producer and with her, this day, was a tall, thin, dark girl with angular eyebrows and elbows who sat rather awkwardly on a fluffy couch and eyed me, when I came in, with the steady indifference of over-twenty for under-twenty.

". . . She's done a couple of things with the Washington Square Players," Miss de Forest was saying, "but we feel that in this London production of *Little Women* she has really hit her stride. She plays 'Jo,' of course." Then, to Father, "Frank, I think you know her father in Buffalo?"

"Of course!" said Pa. "Best-dressed man who ever walked down Delaware Avenue with a boutonniere in his lapel!" Taking notice of me, he added, "Margaret I want you to meet Doctor Cornell's daughter, Kit."

That was my first meeting with Katharine Cornell, memorable because neither of us opened our little traps in the presence of our elders. Miss de Forest told Father about how she had dramatized *Little Women* from the Alcott book, and how Miss Jessie Bonstelle had produced it in London with (I believe) Katharine Cornell the only American in the cast; then she brought out some newspaper reviews from her handbag and read them aloud. All of this was fascinating to Father, who loved any talk about show business, and it naturally interested Miss Cornell and me too. But Father got nervous when any one person talked too long, and pretty soon he began to look around for Bud, who wasn't there. (I forget where Bud was, probably buying old silver in some mews; she was always buying old silver in some mews.) So Father created a diversion by ordering tea, and that was how I came to have my one and only intimate conversation with Katharine Cornell.

"Tea?" I asked.

"Please," said Miss Cornell.

"Sugar?"

"One lump."

"Cream?"

"No, thanks."

End of intimate conversation. Looking back on it now, I realize that Katharine Cornell, in those days, was just as shy as I was. Socially, that is.

On a stage, any stage anywhere, the shyness dropped from her like a discarded cloak and she stepped forth shining with authority. Authority is an actress's power over her audience, the power that, let us say, Helen Hayes exercises like a sorcerer's wand and Ethel Merman wields like a baseball bat. Either way is good, as long as the audience believes in it.

We went to see Miss Cornell in *Little Women* that night, or the next, and her magic reached right over the footlights and took you in charge, just as it does today. I am a notable fusser about the way actresses portray my favorite book heroines (I lay face-down in the aisle and moaned when I saw Shirley Temple as "The Little Colonel"); but, to me, Katharine Cornell's "Jo March" was so entirely perfect that whenever afterward I re-read "Little Women" I always saw "Jo" as Katharine Cornell.

I have not been privileged to know her well since then, but when I do see her, at great intervals, she always seems to me to be one of the few actresses who, offstage, possesses utterly the captivating quality of being interested in *you*. I have never run across her, at a party or even after one of her own first nights, that she hasn't recognized me and said something like, "Well, Margaret, what are you up to these days? I liked that last thing you wrote." And you feel she means it.

Come to think of it, Mrs. Eleanor Roosevelt is about the only other celebrated woman I remember who has this priceless gift. They almost had to pick me up off the floor the day Father introduced me to her in the Algonquin lobby (he always gave me full billing as "my daughter, Margaret Case Harriman"), and Mrs. Roosevelt, with no other clue whatever, said, "Oh, yes! I have so enjoyed reading your Profiles in the New Yorker!" Well, really, now! It was so completely charming and genuine that I very nearly didn't vote for Willkie next election.

Besides meeting old friends in London, we made many new acquaintances, one of whom caused considerable consternation in the family. On the boat coming over we had met an English baronet whom I shall call Sir Lispenard Pim. Sir Lispenard was fiftyish, about five feet five inches tall, and sported a guardsman's mustache so sweeping that it gave him the appearance of bucking against it. He was a charming man, though, and extremely kind to us in London. He was a member of Parliament and took us to lunch in the House, had us to dine at his bachelor's flat in the Albany, and was altogether so attentive that Father and Bud naturally asked him, at last, to dine with us at the Carlton. The date was set for, say, Wednesday night.

Wednesday about six I got home from a thrilling solo trip to Golder's Green, and was reminded by Bud that Sir Lispenard was coming to dine at seven. I repaired to my room to dress, not feeling much enthusiasm.

The only permanent wave of that time was a painful process of yanking, steaming and cooking, and having seen a friend of mine weep and shriek her way through this torture, I had never had a permanent. My hair was long and, except for a remnant of childhood curl around the temples, straight. In addition to these trials, I felt that it was time I wore it *up*, and I had just been allowed to do so. It took me one solid hour to put up my hair in the coiffure I had chosen, a fancy arrangement of three rolls at the back, each of which had to be on an exactly even line with the next. I shudder now to think of the hours I spent pinning up those rolls, taking them down as unsatisfactory, and putting them up again. Father once noticed the strain I was under and gave me a bit of oblique advice, which I ignored.

"Your hair looks fine," he said, "but you are beginning to get lines in your face about it."

The night Sir Lispenard came to dine I was twenty minutes late to dinner, owing to the struggle with the hair, and Father looked at me without pleasure when I finally joined the table. Promptness was one of his courtesies. Dinner passed off well, though, and afterward Bud and I withdrew to our withdrawing room upstairs and left Father and Sir Lispenard to their cigars.

In about half an hour Father came upstairs alone, looking bewildered. "Where is Sir Lispenard?" we asked.

Father sat down, gave me a long look, and then looked at Bud the way a man looks to his wife for strength.

"He thought it would be more delicate to go home, under the circs," he said. "That was the expression he used —'under the circs.'" Father's gaze roved wildly and again rested on me. "My God," he said to Bud, "the man formally asked me for Margaret's hand in marriage."

"*What?*" said Bud, shaken out of her usual calm. They

both started at me with an amazement which I considered less than complimentary. They were no more amazed than I, at that.

"He said," Father continued, "that he had been attracted to Margaret on the ship coming here, but what absolutely bowled him over was the freshness of her Ameddican-gel independence. He exshually, I mean he actually *liked* her being twenty minutes late for dinner."

"What did you tell him, what did you tell him, what did you *tell* him?" I wanted to know quietly.

"I told him it was out of the question, of course, since you are barely seventeen." Father sighed and again gave me the long stare. "It seems *you* told him you were twenty. I pointed out that twenty would be a little young for him, too, and I must say I felt as though I had stabbed him to the heart. The poor fellow just sat there keeping a stiff upper lip until I couldn't stand it any more, and it all ended with me patting him on the shoulder and saying, 'There, there, old chap,' just like Sir Gerald du Maurier in Act Three." Father brightened, as if warmed by an unexpected memory. "By golly," he said, beaming, "I *felt* like Sir Gerald du Maurier in Act Three!"

We never saw Sir Lispenard Pim again, but he was with us in spirit for quite a while. I was naturally intoxicated by my first proposal, however remote, and it made me feel so powerful that, whenever my wishes conflicted with the family's for the next week or so, I would draw myself up and coldly let fall three words: "Lady Pim speaking."

I had to stop it finally because, every time, Father and Bud again focussed on me an unbelieving stare, as if to say, "*This* is Lady Pim?" Father in particular always had a knack of taking me down a peg when I showed signs of swelled head. At the Carlton I had become enamored of

94

the great shining bathroom of our suite with its heated towel rails, and spent hours splashing away in the Carlton's jasmine-scented soap bubbles and carolling *La Gitana*, a favorite air with teatime orchestras that year. To this day, whenever I smell jasmine soap or hear *La Gitana*, I am transported in an instant to the Carlton bathtub in London a million years ago. This dedication to the bath eventually piqued Father, who remarked that anyone would think I had never seen a bathtub before, and didn't I remember that, at home in the Algonquin, I had always had my own private bath?

"Yes, but it hasn't got heated towel rails or jasmine soap!" I pointed out with the cruelty of youth.

"Teddibly sorry," said Father. "The management will be happy to rectify all such omissions on your return, Moddom."

Don't think he forgot, either. The first objects that met my eye on entering my own bathroom when I came home two years later were four filled hot-water bottles draped over the towel rack and two dozen "sample" cakes of Fels-Naphtha laundry soap. Father approved of luxury, all right, but he discouraged fancy ideas in the young.

I think he and Bud were both relieved when the time came to leave London for Paris and to put me back into suitable schoolday, *"tablier noir"* surroundings again. Father, wishing to give his girls every experience, booked passage for Bud and me on the new Handley-Page air service between Croydon Field and Le Bourget airport outside Paris, while he followed by boat with the luggage. Bud and I were, believe it or not, the first women passengers to fly across the English Channel, and got our pictures in the newspapers on the strength of it. Father's pleasure in this exploit was only slightly dimmed by the discovery that, lulled by the motion of the plane, I had slept all the way across and so had missed all of the thrills.

The school Father and Bud had chosen was the *pensionnat* Morel de Fos at Auteuil—a gabled château set in a small park that smelled of cinnamon and pear blossoms and old dogs. Of the two plump spinster sisters who ran it, Mlle. Emilie de Fos was the tough one and Mlle. Marie was the softie; Mlle. Emilie addressed you courteously by your name, but Mlle. Marie never called you anything but *"ma mignonne."* Mlle. Marie was crazy about Americans and, since there were only two in the school beside myself, I was given the honored seat on her right, at table. This, while pleasant, had its disadvantages, especially when we had fish—which was several times a week. The waitress would serve Mlle. Marie first and then go around the table to the left, and by the time the platter got back to me there was never a blooming thing left of those fish but the heads. I lived on fish heads for two years, and gained ten pounds.

The other two Americans were Audrey and Jo. Audrey, a strikingly beautiful and dashing brunette, taught me some mildly naughty French songs, one of which began,

> *Je veux mourir,*
> *O, ma déese!*

and, surprisingly, turned out to be *Some of These Days.* She also told me—in French, since we were not allowed to speak English except on Sundays—all about how a guide in her father's fishing camp, the summer before, had taken her out in a canoe and kissed her hand all the way from the finger tips up to the elbow, and had then tried to cast himself into the lake as being unworthy. I was not surprised to hear, some years later, that the sensational Audrey Emery had married Grand Duke Dmitri of Russia. Compared to Audrey, Jo Hartford was rather quiet and reserved, and talked little about herself or her family. Although we were good friends, it was several years after we left school that I accidentally learned that the Hartfords merely own the entire A. & P. chain of grocery stores.

The bathing arrangements *chez* Mlles. Morel de Fos were quite a comedown from the Carlton Hotel in London. Two tin tubs in the cellar, next to the coalbin, supplied baths to all of the eighty or ninety girls in the school. Naturally, an elaborate system of rotation was necessary, and you were apt to get your weekly tub anywhere from six o'clock in the morning to just before lights-out. Things were a little simplified, however, by the fact that many of the French, Greek, Turkish, Czech and Armenian pupils were willing to trade their bath hours for some trinket or favor more to their liking, so that the tub-happy British and Americans sometimes got as many as two baths a week. Even so, with Annette or Phillipine generally rooting around in the adjacent coalbin and sending a fine spray of soot over the partition, we were like as not to emerge from the water, not white, but a lovely shade of French gray. I suppose I wasn't really clean for two years, but like the fish heads, it seemed to agree with me.

I had a little dormer room of my own on the third floor, with Audrey and a Roumanian girl named Annie Filitti in a big room next door and two English sisters, May and Vera Bostock, on the other side. Annie and May both studied singing, and each naturally wanted to sing in a foreign tongue. When they practiced in their rooms I got it from right and left. From Annie:

> "Pale honts I loave
> Beside ze Shalima-ar . . ."

And from May:

> *"Bel-luh nuwee, oh nuwee d'ahmoor . . .*
> *Nuwee ploo bel-luh quh-huh le joor . . ."*

Generally, however, I was myself incarcerated, during practice periods, at a piano in one of a row of little cells off the *galerie d'hiver* downstairs. These soundproof cells contained nothing but a piano, a stool, the music and the pupil, and the pupil was locked in; nor were they so soundproof, I regret to say, that Mlle. Emilie ever failed to detect it when I abandoned Chopin or Debussy for a little relaxation in the company of Gershwin or Berlin. She would come trotting up, her enormous bunch of keys jingling at her waist, rap smartly on the glass-panelled door and make faces at me. I later found out she was saying, *"Quelle horreur est-ce que vous faites là, Marguerite?"* My popular music came in handy most evenings, though, when we all danced in the *galerie d'hiver*. In fact, I was so steadily employed at the piano that I never got a chance to dance, and to this day I can't "lead" worth a hoot. There was one very fat Turkish girl named Zaidée who was particularly mad about American jazz, and on Sundays I taught her to sing a few songs, Al Jolson style. I have a warm memory of the Terrible Turk down on one knee with arms outstretched, coon-shouting:

> "Swa-anee! HOW I loaf you, HOW I loaf you!
> MY dear old Swanee!"

In return, Zaidée taught me her own refinements of the French language. It was not proper, she said, merely to say "*Merci*" when one wanted no more of a certain dish at dinner; the thing to say was, "*Merci, je suis rassasiée.*" The first time I produced this remark at the table the French girls held their napkins to their mouths to stifle their giggles, and *ces dames* looked at me curiously. After dinner I cornered a French girl and found out that, whereas "*Merci*" means "No, thank you," Zaidée's phrase, "*Merci, je suis rassasiée,*" means "Thanks to you, I am glutted and cloyed." Darkly, I sought out the Terrible Turk and confronted her with her fancy French. She shrugged her shoulders and smiled.

"In Turkey, it is a compliment," she explained.

Probably everyone's boarding-school recollections are largely concerned with eating. . . . I know mine are. Every morning for breakfast, *chez* Morel de Fos, we had a blissful kind of white honey I had never tasted before. We never had toast, of course, and very little butter, but this honey spread on thick slices of a soft, rather coarse bread, was the best thing I had ever eaten. For years after I came home I haunted food shops looking for this magic honey, but nobody had ever heard of it until, one day in a Third Avenue delicatessen, I spotted two jars of it in a carton on the counter.

"I want those!" I shouted. "I don't care if you've sold them to somebody else, I must have them!"

The clerk peered into the carton, and then at me. "Are you crazy?" he inquired. "That's just honey that's gone bad and turned into sugar. We were about to throw it away."

He gave the two jars to me, shaking his head, and I hurried home and spread some of the honey on a thick slice of bread. It didn't taste the way it tasted when I was seventeen.

99

Now that I haven't touched a sweet in ten years, no longer caring for them (and maybe the delicatessen honey had something to do with it), it astonishes me to remember how we used to pack them in at school in France. At recess, twice a day, old Annette would roam the garden paths with a huge basket on her arm, calling out *"Bouchées au caramel! Su-u-ucre d'orge!"* and we would almost knock one another down to get to her, our grimy little French-gray hands holding out coppers or, with the rich and greedy, sometimes a whole franc note. Annette's chocolate-covered caramels were much more than a bouchée, or mouthful. They stretched the mouth deliciously so that any two persons engaged with *bouchées* were obliged to communicate with each other by hilarious pantomime. Her *sucre d'orge* was simpler, just a stick of barley sugar which could be broken up, stickily concealed in a *cahier*, and unobtrusively sucked on during the next class.

It seems strange, doesn't it, that girls of seventeen should have acted so much like children in the 'twenties? It's true, though. Except in special cases noted by Scott Fitzgerald, seventeen-year-olds were considered to be children during the 'twenties. And in France, where girls were chaperoned until they were married, seventeen was even younger than it was in America.

I approve of this thoroughly, and will never cease to be grateful that I missed a good deal of the Jazz Age because I was in France. In the years between, I know of only one woman who was really involved in the Jazz Age and who survived it, and that is Constance Bennett. But she is made of duralumin.

To get back to food: on Fridays, the pupils of Mlles. Morel de Fos used to march down, double file, to Auteil, where we were free to buy whatever we wished according to our allowances. The patisserie was our goal. Eclairs, mille-feuilles, babas, and a tremendous thing I forget the name of . . . six inches high, it was, made of coffee frosting and filled with mocha cream, with whipped cream and a maraschino cherry on top. We struggled home carrying these creations carefully before us, and placed them on the top shelf of the *armoire* in our rooms, for later feasting. This led to a lively company of uninvited pets in our rooms. One night I heard a scrabbling sound after lights-out. I lit the candle given to us in case of emergency and beheld, trying to get into the *armoire*, the first and (I hope) only large rat I have ever seen. It was as big as a buck rabbit.

I screamed, and the rat, startled, ran toward the door. I jumped out of bed, opened the door, and kicked him into the hall. It was unfortunate that he landed on the bosom of Miss Emilie, who was just coming upstairs to bed.

There was a conference next morning: result, no more food in *armoires*. All *armoires* were washed out with lye soap, with the result that our hats dissolved. But at least we didn't have any more rats in the rooms . . . or, alas, any more pastries in the *armoires*.

Saturdays were even better than Fridays. On Saturday, we marched two-by-two to the Metro, with a teacher, and were whisked into Paris to do our shopping, or on great occasions to go to the *Comédie Francaise* or the *Opéra Comique*. The autumn theatre season coincided with the autumn rains, and we would come up from the Metro with umbrellas poised, and struggle against the wind and pouring rain until we got to the theatre. Personally, I never thought the French theatre was worth it. It seemed terribly affected to me, after the natural kind of American theatre I had already seen with my father. Racine and Molière passed unnoticed before my eyes, while I wondered what kind of pastry I was going to have for tea.

We always had tea, on Saturdays *chez* Colombin in the rue Cambon. "Tea," of course, really meant all kinds of great thick gooey cakes, and hot chocolate with whipped cream. Colombin is still there, I discover every time I go back to Paris, and I always pay it a wistful visit. But I can't eat those gooey cakes any more. I settle for a cup of coffee and a croissant.

The last time I was there, a year or so ago, I got so carried away by memories that I said, in French, to an elderly waitress, "You know, I used to come here when I was in school at Auteuil."

"Oh?" the waitress replied in English. "That must have been many years ago."

"I'll kill her. I'll kill her!" I said, rising from the table. Only Germaine, sitting beside me, restrained me from a simple murder on the spot.

But . . . *ou sont les neiges d'antin?* You might as well search for last year's snow as get mad because you can't find it.

Summers were wonderful, in France. One summer holiday six of us—French and English girls, with me the only American—went to Dinard, in Brittany, chaperoned by Miss Ives, the school's English mistress. Miss Ives was a small British spinster straight from the pages of Katharine Mansfield: the worn felt toque, the tired fur tippet, the hopeful, hopeless darting of the busy hands that never did anything quite right. Miss Ives had lived twenty years in France, but she was so thoroughly loyal to England that

Vasiliu

she declined to speak French with anything but a British accent.

"Regahday lay petty woyzo, mays ongfong," she would remark as she promenaded us, two by two, in the Parc des Princes, near the school. This meant, *"Regardez les petits oiseaux, mes enfants,"* and it had the immediate effect of making us wish to break ranks and kick all birds to death.

Although she was so firmly British, Miss Ives had a thoroughly French respect for anybody with money, and at Dinard she actually allowed a rich and dashing South American gentleman with a handsome car to take us all to tea, and for occasional drives. One day he drove us to Mont-Saint-Michel, and he and I sat on a rock a little apart from Miss Ives and the other girls while he told me that his emotions concerning me were like the famous Mont-Saint-Michel tide that came rushing in faster than galloping horses. *"C'est plus fort que moi, même que nous deux,"* he said. I am so immodest as to mention this (so soon after Sir Lispenard Pim) only because it illustrates how closely akin most languages are. Years afterward, I recognized a ghostly echo of my South American, the first time I heard a radio comedian say, "It's bigger than the both of us."

The next summer, I visited a schoolmate named Rosemary in Scotland and met my first real live lord in person. He was Rosemary's grandfather, Lord Leith, and he lived in Fyvie Castle in Aberdeenshire, which was where I went to visit Rosemary. Lord Leith had married an American, a Miss January (yes, really) of New York, and they were both absolute darlings, right out of P. G. Wodehouse.

"I *say*, that's a pretty hat you've got on!" said Lord Leith to me one day. "Take it off."

I took it off, because after all I was eighteen and he was

eighty, and I was a guest. But I soon found out that no Scottish lord ever gives an order without a reason. Lord Leith was taking me out to see the bulls.

"Your hat is red, you see," he explained as we walked across the park to the bull pasture, "and you never can tell how these fellows will take it if you move. They don't mind the color red, you know, it's only the movement they mind."

We came up to the bull pasture where about a dozen cross-looking beasts were frowning at us. "Would you like to see these fellows really annoyed?" Lord Leith asked me. Without waiting for my answer, he pulled a scarlet bandana out of his pocket and waved it at the bulls. They charged us. I can still hear the pounding of their hoofs on the turf, I can still see the angry red eyes looking up at us as they charged, head down.

"Silly animals," said Lord Leith, turning his back on them. "Let's go back and have some tea."

And, believe me or not, those bulls stopped dead, and went back to grazing. I guess I knew then, if I had never known it before, that nobody can ever lick the British or the Scotch. They just don't pay any *attention* to anybody who is trying to kill them.

Lady Leith was upset about the bull episode, and plied me with muffins and jam and extra-strong tea. "One day you'll go too *far* with those animals!" she scolded her husband.

After I was in bed that night Rosemary came into my room. "Well, you passed the test," she said. "Grandfather does that to everybody who comes here, and usually they scream, or run, and try to climb a tree. Apparently you just stood still. Grandfather *likes* that."

"I'm glad," I said weakly. I thought it unnecessary to explain that I had been too paralyzed with fright to move a muscle.

The next morning when the maid brought me my hot, weak tea, I looked around my great, cold bedroom, and another truth occurred to me. "Now I know," I said to myself, "why the British have to have a cup of tea before they get out of bed. It's to thaw them out before they have to freeze again." I got of bed, shivering, dressed, went downstairs and had breakfast, and made another great discovery.

It's only *castles* that are cold.

Rosemary and I went for a walk across the moor after breakfast. The sun was hot, the heather was in bloom, and a little silvery stream was running nowhere in particular. We took off our shoes and stockings and waded in the water, and walked through the heather barefoot.

If you have never walked through the heather barefoot in Scotland you have never done anything.

"Oh, I *love* this country!" I shouted, bursting in for lunch.

Lady Leith smiled. "I knew you would," she said. "It takes a little time."

"And after lunch," said Lord Leith, beaming, "I'll take you to see the pigs!"

From Scotland I went back to England to visit some friends of Father's in Kent, and accidentally stumbled onto a whole blessed day alone in London. Father's friends put me on the train with the understanding that I was to meet Miss Ives at The Girls' Friendly Society in London, from which admirable haven she would escort me back to school in France. Arriving at the Girls' Friendly,

I learned that Miss Ives' boat train had been held up for twenty-four hours, and she would not be there until the next day.

Well! If you were eighteen years old and loose in London, would you hole up at the Girls' Friendly? Nor would I. Like the arrow from the bow I went to the Carlton Hotel, explained that I was the daughter of Frank Case of the Algonquin in New York, and would they please give me a suite and charge it to Father? They did.

From my luxurious apartment I telephoned everybody I knew within ten miles and said, "I'm having a tea party tomorrow at the Carlton, do come!" Then I called the Girls' Friendly and left word for Miss Ives to pick me up at the Carlton. When she arrived the next afternoon, the suite was bursting with a dozen girls having tea, scones, hot buttered muffins, jam, jelly, ices, French pastry, and ice-cream sodas, and Miss Ives and I barely made the evening boat train to Paris.

This cosy inspiration cost Father about fifteen pounds, English money, but after a little grumbling via transatlantic mail, he enjoyed it as much as we did. Partly because we had fun, which he always approved of, and partly because the Carlton in London never for a moment questioned his daughter's right to charge a suite and a high tea to him. Father had a wonderful naïveté about himself; he was always pleased and surprised when people recognized him as a well-known man.

Miss Ives didn't feel so happy about it. "Well, vraymong, Margareet," she kept saying all the way back to Paris, "vooz ate oon tray maychante joon fee!"

I knew I wasn't in any real trouble, though, when Mlle. Marie met us at the door, kissed me lightly, and said, "Ah! Ma mignonne!"

I have been in France many times since I went to school there, but I somehow never got around to revisiting the *pensionnat* Morel de Fos until 1936 when, overtaken by nostalgia, I made a solitary pilgrimage to the scenes of my youth.

Autueil, and the neighborhood around the Parc des Princes, was so crowded with new apartment houses that my driver had trouble locating Number 3, rue du Pavillon, which was the school's street address. When we finally drew up in front of it, I stared in dismay at the rusty gate and the once-beautiful grounds inside. Where was my little park, where were the rustic bridge, the summerhouse, the gay flower beds? The place was a choked wilderness, struggling against a concrete tide of modernistic community dwellings with chrome staircases spilling like lost viscera down their fronts and sides. It was hideous beyond belief.

I could see figures moving at the windows of the château, however, so I got out and rang the concierge's bell. No concierge appeared, even after my second and third attempts, so I wandered down to the corner where an ancient workman was raking leaves. I asked him where the concierge was, and how I could get into 3 rue du Pavillon. He raised his shoulders and let them fall.

"But I must get in! I have come all the way from Paris to visit this house!" I told him. "*Il faut que j'y entre! Il faut, il faut,* IL FAUT!" I yelled, and then I began jumping up and down.

My particular form of intensity goes great with French people. When Mother gets excited, they really drop everything. My ancient gardener abandoned his rake and clasped his hands sympathetically.

"*Oh, la pauvre dame!*" he exclaimed. He signalled me

to follow him through a swamp and a brier patch and finally delivered me, breathless and torn, at the front door. I thanked him, gave him five francs, pulled the bell, and was admitted.

The great entrance hall was filled with telephone switchboards operated by busy young women, and there were several nervous-looking young men pacing back and forth across the marble floor under the very noses of Psyche and Adonis, the busts I remembered so well, which still stood at the entrance to the *parloir*. After one astonished look I approached one of the telephone operators.

"What is it, then, that this establishment now finds itself?" I inquired.

"But, see you, madame," the operator replied, "it is a lying-in hospital."

As I left the *maison d'accouchement* I saw my little gardener again, leaning on his rake. I waved him a melancholy farewell and he stared at me in amazement. "*Déjà?*" he said.

"No wonder he thought I was in such a hurry to get in there," I reflected as I climbed into my taxi and rode sadly back to Paris.

* Chapter 5 *

I CAME home from school in France at the height of the Jazz Age, and it almost threw me for a while. All the boys I had left strumming guitars in the moonlight were toting flasks and comparing bootleggers, and many of the girls I knew—with a few notable exceptions—were eloping, or had already been married and annulled. New York, in the 'twenties, was a startling place to a girl fresh from the decorum of a French boarding school.

I didn't drink, or smoke, and I had to have "necking" explained to me, which amused the other girls and depressed the boys. I was in danger of being a social failure, a complete dud, or (as it was called in those days) a "wet smack."

The only thing I could do was dance, so I threw myself into the career of a prom girl. I went to every college prom I was asked to, and for about six months my chief concern was whether I would be cut in on as often as Connie Bennett or Buff Cobb (the one and only original Buff Cobb), or whether—oh, heaven!—I could get as many stags trailing me around the floor as those two girls had. Presently Father said, "I think you ought to have a coming-out party," and he and Bud put their heads together with the usual stunning effect.

Paul Whiteman, in person, led the orchestra for my party. The tables were taken out of the Oak Room and the Chinese Room in the Algonk, and we danced all the way from Forty-fourth Street practically to Forty-fifth. There were favors, balloons and bells. I remember Father being enchanted by one girl, Dorothy Stuart, who fastened her bells around her ankle so that she jingled as she danced.

There was a fruit punch and lots of food. There was (it occurs to me now) no liquor, and there were no cigarettes. But Georges, the headwaiter, had to blink the lights three times and finally turn them out before the kids would go home.

Now, a thousand parties later, I still think it was the best party I ever saw.

Having been successfully launched in the social world —our own social world, that is—I naturally wanted something else. I had not forgotten Thomas Chatterton in his attic in Bloomsbury or Holborn or wherever, and I wished to be a writer. Following the opposite direction from Thomas Chatterton's attic, I took the subway to Park Row and applied for a job at every newspaper on the street, being regularly thrown out until I reached the *American* —now the *Journal-American*.

The editor of the Sunday Magazine Section read my application card, looked up at me, and said, "Your name is Case, you live at the Algonquin, you ought to get us some good juicy stories. Go home and bring me some real hot gossip about Douglas Fairbanks, or Ina Claire, or whoever you can get the inside stuff on."

I wanted the job, but I hated this man. I drew myself

up to my full height and replied, "Those people are my father's friends. Even if I *knew* any gossip about them I wouldn't write it."

"Good-bye," said the Sunday editor.

Finally I got to see the city editor of the *Globe*, and he tried me out on a fat assignment. "Go write me a story about what's happening on the corner of Forty-second Street and Times Square," he ordered. I took off, and dithered for an hour on all four corners of Times Square which, to my nineteen-year-old, city-bred gaze, appeared about the same as usual. I came back and looked the city ed in the eye.

"*Nothing*," I told him, "is happening on the corner of Forty-second Street and Times Square."

"You'll do," he said, and thereafter sent me out on some very satisfying feature stories; backstage at the Metropolitan, the opening of the first big radio stations, the last fire horse in the world still operating at an enginehouse in Queens. . . . The *Globe* paid me ten dollars a column and usually gave two columns to my pieces three times a week, so (although I had no by-line) I was soon making sixty dollars a week. Father was enchanted.

He clipped all my pieces out of the paper and followed people around the Algonquin lobby, shoving the clips at them. "*Margaret* wrote this!" he would say with an air of pleased astonishment which most of his friends kindly shared, but he came up against trouble when he tried to make his old buddy, Douglas Fairbanks, read my written works. Mr. Fairbanks, as I have intimated in a former book, was allergic to the printed word. As Father once said to him, after lending him a book cunningly marked with paper slips and receiving it back in the exact same condition, "It isn't as though you *couldn't* read, Doug,—or *can* you?" My own theory, that Douglas simply didn't want to sit still long enough to read anything, was fairly proved when Father, failing to capture him in the lobby, eventually pinned him down in the family apartment upstairs and thrust one of my *Globe* pieces into his hands. "Margaret wrote this. Read it," he ordered.

Douglas, huddled in a chair, "read" the two columns in ten seconds (you could tell from his wildly darting eye that the printed message wasn't reaching him), and then he bounced out of the chair and said, "Gee, Frank, that's wonderful! Gee, Margaret, that's swell! I better get downstairs and get to bed now, it's pretty late." In the doorway he turned, and for once failed to flash his famous smile. "I've had trouble getting to sleep lately," he said.

"Oh?" said Father icily. "Would you care for something to read?"

The *Globe* folded a month or so after I went to work for it (any witticisms would be gratuitous, thank you; in other words no cheap cracks, kids), and again I took to the subways looking for a job. Once more the job came to me from a stranger, and not any on the subway circuit either. Henriette Metcalf, drama editor of *Vanity Fair* was going to Europe for six weeks and called me up to ask if I would pinch-hit for her while she was away. Mrs. Metcalf never came home, as far as I knew, and I stayed at *Vanity Fair* for six wonderful years. *Vanity Fair* was, along with its sister publication, *Vogue*, the slickest and most fashionable magazine of that time, shortly before the advent of *The New Yorker*. I have worked for both magazines, and it seems strange that my over-all recollection of each is that *Vanity Fair* editors (of whom I shall have more to say in the next chapter) walked lightly along the corridors, and *New Yorker* editors walk heavy.

I imagine that Father and I, who were always pretty pleased with each other, never got more mutual pleasure than we did from my first two, unheralded, jobs. The very first one, the *Globe* assignments, I announced in the traditional manner by handing Father a copy of the paper at dinner one evening with a request to "read this piece and see what you think of it." Just like Jo, in "Little Women," remember? When a newspaper printed Jo's first story she nonchalantly read it aloud to Meg, Beth, and Amy without revealing the author's name, and when they admired it and asked who had written it, Jo "suddenly sat up very straight, displayed a flushed countenance, and replied in a loud voice, 'Your sister!'" (I'm quoting from memory.) Naturally, I did none of these things; after all, Jo had an edge on me, she had a by-line. Nor did Father flutter around me like the March sisters when I modestly said, "*I* wrote it." What he did was much more exciting, to me. He left his dinner—his favorite dinner of rare roast beef and hashed-in-cream potatoes—and streaked out to the newsstand to buy all the *Globes* they had. He could have sent a bus boy, or a bell boy, you know. After he got back to the table, looking like a newsvendor, no customer was safe who did not immediately wish to read an unsigned piece about something or other in that evening's *Globe*.

What I remember mostly about that evening, however, was the surprised, delighted stare Father gave me when I told him I had written the piece in the paper. I wanted to keep it that way. When you have a father you love who suddenly looks at you in surprise and delight, I guess you always want to keep it that way. Therefore, my next announcement at dinner, about the *Vanity Fair* job, was made in a skeptical tone. After all, Father knew Condé Nast, the publisher of *Vanity Fair*, and Frank Crowninshield, its editor. "Father," I asked him in a rather intense way, "did you have anything to do with the job I got today?"

"What job?" Father asked, and a look at his face convinced me that this was news to him.

"I'm drama editor on *Vanity Fair*, beginning tomorrow," I said.

Once again we gazed upon each other in mutual pleasure and satisfaction, and if Father's delight was slightly tempered this time, I now know why. To Father, a young person's accomplishment was either something he could watch on a stage or read in print. The mere fact of getting an executive job seemed less than sensational to him—after all, he had an executive job himself. What he wanted from youth was a picture he could hold in his mind and heart, the kind of picture that was given to him when he went to the theatre or read a book. People who acted or wrote were people he loved; those who were only connected in an executive way with actors and writers he considered as so much fringe—some kind of agents, maybe. And now he was faced with a daughter who had become a part of that fringe.

He was fine about it, though. He even wrote Frank Crowninshield a letter of reassurance next day, as follows:

> Dear Frank:
> My daughter Margaret tells me that she has gone to work for you on *Vanity Fair*. She is a good girl and will do a great job. Just keep the matches away from her.
>
> Frank

Crowny's reply was equally hopeful:

Dear Frank:

We are enjoying Margaret. We hope to enjoy her even more by next Tuesday, when we take her leg-chains off.

Frank

For a couple of years after returning from France I lived a full life while scarcely ever leaving one city block —Forty-fourth Street, between Fifth and Sixth Avenues. My home was at the Algonquin (59 West 44 Street) and I worked at *Vanity Fair*, which was then at 19 West 44 Street. I was in no way chained to this block, and frequently took off for proms and other out-of-town parties, but these trips were strictly diversions. Life on Forty-fourth Street was so complete that it was unnecessary to look any further for new interests.

It was quite a street. Even beyond my own block, and all the way from Grand Central Terminal to Eighth Avenue, it was a striking thoroughfare. On the northeast corner of Fifth Avenue was Delmonico's, where I had attended Miss Robinson's dancing classes (or were they Professor Dodsworth's?) and pointed my toes to the tune of *Narcissus* . . . da-DUM, da-DUM, da-da-de-ah-da-da-DUM. On the southeast corner stood the Harriman National Bank, whose president I had never met, although I was later to marry his cousin Oliver's son. Across Fifth Avenue *our* block began with the old Fifth Avenue Bank on the northwest corner and Sherry's on the southwest, where the Guaranty Trust now stands—at least, where it stands as I write this; in New York you never know these days. Continuing west on Forty-fourth you found the Harvard Club, the New York Yacht Club, the City Club, the Bar Association, the Algonquin, the Rocky Mountain Club (which occupied the old Fred Thompson apartment in the Algonquin Annex) and, on the corner of Sixth Avenue, the beloved Hippodrome. R. H. Burnside, the Hippodrome's manager, had always given me a box for each new "spectacle" and, on two occasions, my little friends and I provided a small spectacle of our own. One occurred when Elizabeth Baskerville, sister of the painter Charles Baskerville, got so carried away by the show that she fell out of the box and had to be hauled back by her blue taffeta sash, and the other when we took along a box of hard candies and, during intermission, tried to see how accurately we could fire them at a compellingly bald gentleman seated below.

Father's theatre manners were impeccable—he was the only man I ever knew who always rolled up the taxi-windows on the way to a theatre so that a girl's hair would not be blown, and who invariably handed you the playbill correctly folded to the program of the evening—and fortunately my own manners improved in time for him to take me to my first opening night, at the Hudson Theatre, west of Sixth Avenue on Forty-fourth. (We're still strolling along Forty-fourth Street, with your permission.) The new play was a romantic comedy called *He Comes Up Smiling* and it starred Douglas Fairbanks who, I vividly remember, made his first entrance leaping over a garden wall to join his leading lady, a young ingenue named Patricia Collinge. The Hudson was next door to the famed Belasco Theatre where, among many other performances, I saw Lionel Atwill as "Debureau," and the unforgettable Lenore Ulric as "Kiki." Not long ago I went to a movie featuring a big ballroom scene, and among the guests in the crowd around the buffet was Lenore Ulric. She had one line: "Lovely party, isn't it?" or something like that. As for the dear Hudson Theatre . . . *eheu!* You guessed it. It is now a television studio.

Proceeding west along Forty-fourth (lean on *me*, grandfather) and crossing the street, we come to one of the most famous actors' clubs in America, The Lambs. Any Lamb will tell you that this club must be called "The Lambs" and not "The Lambs Club" as ignoramuses sometimes refer to it; Father, one of its few layman members and for some years a member of the Council, always painstakingly corrected clods who made this mistake. The Lambs, he pointed out, was originally named for Charles and Mary Lamb who held such spirited soirées in nineteenth-century London that the general cry from anyone bored with customary pursuits and thirsting for mental stimulation, was "Let's go round to the Lambs'!" Charles and Mary apparently enjoyed this reaction (just as my father loved hearing people say automatically, "I'll meet you at the Algonk,"), for when they died they left a house they owned on the Thames to the use of actors and writers so that these emotional orphans might still say, "Let's go round to the Lambs'." In 1874, a lonely and now forgotten English actor named Henry J. Montague stood on a New York street corner (possibly Forty-fourth Street) with a couple of other actors who also had no place to go.

"Let's go around to the Lambs'," Mr. Montague said bitterly.

"Why not?" said George H. McLean, one of his companions.

"Why not, indeed? We'll organize our own Lambs' right here!" said Arthur Wallack, the third member of the trio, whose son, Lester Wallack, was to become a famous actor and have a theatre named after him.

Then and there, with the help of some other lonesome

actors, the Lambs was organized. For many years the Lambs held an honorable position among actors' clubs; Lambs considered members of the Players' Club to be stuffed shirts, and members of the Friars' Club to be upstarts; somewhat in the same way that the Racquet Club considers the Knickerbocker Club dull, and the New York Athletic Club beneath comment. The Lambs was a lively club for legitimate stage actors, and I had an inkling of its decline only when Father came home one day from a council meeting, picked up his crossword-puzzle book, and asked me for a two-letter word meaning sun god. He knew as well as I did that the only crossword sun god was Ra, so I said, "What's the matter Pa, or Ra? What upset you at the Lambs?"

Father closed his puzzle book, put his pencil back in the ruby-glass jar, rose from his chair, and paced the room. Finally he stopped in front of me.

"They've got *radio* actors in there!" he said.

Darling Father. He loved the theatre, he understood the work that went into making an actor or an actress, and he was always there to see their success—the most excited guy in the audience. He couldn't stand it when an actor became merely a voice on radio.

In spite of his moony love for the theatre, and for actors and actresses, Father reared like a frightened colt when, on one of his visits to California, Douglas Fairbanks suggested that he play the part of the sheriff in the current Fairbanks picture. "You can ride, and you've certainly got the eagle eye and the hawk nose for the part," Douglas reminded him urgently. Father declined, but I always thought he was rather tempted.

As for me, I never had any desire to go into pictures, or on the stage. I say it apologetically, aware of how many girls would have given the world for my opportunities and my contacts through Father's friends in the theatre. The simple truth is that I wanted to work on a newspaper or a magazine and had no yearning, and almost certainly no talent, to be an actress. Possibly I was conditioned by my one effort, some years earlier, in a Gardner School production of *Iphigenia in Aulis* in which I was given the role of a Greek maiden whose only line was, "What is in this precious flask?" Owing to a slight lisp I suffered from at the time, I kept saying, "What ish in zish preshush flashk?" and after the second rehearsal the coach took my line away from me and put me in the chorus of garlanded, but silent, Greek dancers.

Mr. Fairbanks had an occasional random notion that I ought to be in the movies, and he would sometimes make me stand shoulder to shoulder with him while he nervously asked Father, "Is she as tall as I am? Is she *almost* as tall?" I was two or three inches shorter, but that was not tiny enough for a movie heroine of that era who was supposed to gaze adoringly up at the hero from the vicinity of his top waistcoat button. Nothing ever came of the idea, and the careers of Marguerite De La Motte, Bebe Daniels and other Fairbanks leading ladies remained unthreatened by me.

Rudolph Valentino was the only man who ever got me anywhere near show business in a professional way. As drama editor of *Vanity Fair*, I assembled the theatre pages, wrote the captions, and escorted actors and actresses to Edward Steichen's studio to be photographed for the magazine. Naturally, when Valentino came to town he was good for a full-page picture, and it was when we were returning from the studio that he asked me if I had ever thought of acting in movies. I said no, and he asked me to lunch with him and his wife the following day. We had lunch in the sitting room of their suite in (I think) the Vanderbilt Hotel, and for a while I was too much interested in observing them both to wonder why I was there. Valentino was a handsome, highly agreeable, sensible, somewhat humorless young man who showed, in person, little of the electric quality that vibrated from him on the screen. His wife was much more dramatic. Natacha Rambova, née Winifred Hudnut, was a compelling brunette with camellia-white skin and long, startling eyes, who always wore tight-bodiced gowns that fell in rich folds to her ankles. (In that period of knee-length skirts it was rumored, of course, that she had thick legs and ankles, but I never found out whether this was true.)

They were delightful hosts, but a little nerve-wracking because of the peculiar interest they took in me that day. Miss Rambova, leaning her chin upon a white hand, would stare at me unblinking for a minute and a half, and then she would get up, go around back of my chair, and stare at me from the other side. Meanwhile Valentino kept darting out of *his* chair, squatting on his haunches, and peering at me from various angles through circles made by thumb and forefinger around each eye. Once more seated at the table, he would raise an eyebrow at his wife and ask, "What do you think?" Miss Rambova would nod slowly and murmur, "Possible. It's possible."

With dessert they let me in on the big news. "I am about to make *Monsieur Beaucaire*," Valentino told me, "and I would like to test you for the part of—but surely you know which part I have in mind?"

This was a staggerer. I had lovingly read and reread every word that Booth Tarkington ever wrote, with one exception; owing to an indifference toward romantic cos-

tume fiction, I had never read *Monsieur Beaucaire*. I said so, and my hosts looked at me as though I had announced that I didn't know how to sign my name. They explained kindly, however, that the part was that of Lady Mary Carlisle, who is in love with Beaucaire.

"She is a great English lady, and you look ladylike," said Valentino simply. He had, always, a most engaging simplicity of thought and expression.

"I'm pretty tall," I reminded him.

"No matter. You will do all of your scenes with me sitting down—('*Lying* down is more like it,' interpolated Miss Rambova)—and anyway, to be tall will make you look more regal."

I said I would have to ask Father since I was still under age, thanked them, and rushed home with the great tidings. Father, quite excited, said, "Sure, go ahead, what can you lose?" A date was set for the test and at the appointed time, after an intense morning at the hairdresser's, I presented myself at the studio, an old building on Sixth Avenue. Valentino was there with a cameraman, a director, and a couple of assistants and we first made several shots of the two of us together, to determine my height and whether my best profile interfered with Valentino's best profile, and so on. This was no strain whatever, and I laughingly said as much to one and all. Then came my big moment—my solo test, my chance to reveal what a great actress I was.

The scene they gave me to act out was, I suppose, a stock scene handed to all novices, but if they had dredged it up out of Edgar Allan Poe, it couldn't have horrified me more. I was to enter a room, find a letter on the table, open and read it, and then disclose to the audience by means of gestures and facial expressions that this letter contained the news that my lover had just been killed in an avalanche.

I am certain that the performance I gave that afternoon would, on some later day, have won me the Gary Cooper Award for restrained acting. Unfortunately, for the school of histrionics then in vogue on the silver screen, it was decidedly understated. I entered the room all right, gave the slight start prescribed by the director upon finding the letter, read the fateful message and then stood there wearing an expression of faint regret, like a Junior Miss on being told that she cannot have another new party dress until the first of the year.

A gracious Providence (or perhaps an equally gracious Valentino) protected me from ever seeing that test. Doris Kenyon was engaged to play the Lady Mary and I was forced to admit, when I saw the picture, that she did it quite well.

I saw Valentino again before he went back to the Coast, when I asked him and his wife to lunch at the Algonquin one day. Miss Rambova couldn't come, but Valentino turned up with his manager and that is the only time I remember witnessing scenes of positive turmoil in the notoriously blasé Algonquin Rose Room. The Rose Room was so famous a meeting place for celebrities that a peevish actor once remarked that a man would have to cut his throat, die, and be resurrected whole before their very eyes in order to attract any attention. On this day attendance was normal. The members of the Algonquin Round Table were lunching, as usual, in the rear center of the room—Robert Benchley, Dorothy Parker, Heywood Broun, Franklin P. Adams, Marc Connelly, George S. Kaufman, Alexander Woollcott and the rest. I don't remember exactly who occupied the other tables but, since it was an average day, the patrons probably included Constance Collier, Gertrude Atherton, Carl Van Vechten, Judith Anderson, Basil Rathbone, Estelle Winwood, Walter Hampden, Laurette Taylor, and a few Drews and Barrymores among others. What I do remember is the buzz of excitement that ran through the room at the sight of Valentino; you could hear it vibrate from one of these ordinarily unimpressionable groups to the next. Alex Woollcott made one of his fast, pivot turns in his chair and gave Valentino a long look before he swung back to his normal, or eating, position. Gertrude Atherton and Constance Collier ate most of their lunch with their lorgnettes focussed on Rudy. Carl Van Vechten, seated near us, made faces at me over Valentino's shoulder because his wife, Fania Marinoff, was going through swooning motions at his side. People in the lobby, hearing news of The Presence, crowded into the entrance of the Rose Room to take a peek. Nobody came up and asked for an autograph—that was against the Algonquin rule—but no celebrity, before or since, ever made such a sensation in the Algonk Rose Room as Valentino did.

As for me, I was The Most Popular Girl at the Ball. More people came to our table in an hour and tenderly inquired about my health than had given a hoot about it in the past twelve months. When the traffic got really thick, I began to feel slightly apologetic, and I asked Mr. Valentino if he minded.

"Mind?" he said, happily cutting into his creamed chicken pancake, "I love it. I would be a fool if I didn't."

This was in considerable contrast to Douglas Fairbanks, who privately referred to his fans and autograph hunters as "boll-weevils."

Presently, calm and refreshing as always, came Father.

I said, "Father, this is Mr. Valentino . . . my father, Frank Case." Before I could introduce Valentino's manager, Valentino's manager sternly corrected me.

"Mr. Valentino, may I *present* Mr. Frank Case," he said.

Valentino gave this manager a look Agnes Ayres never received. I had the impression that it conveyed a distinct kick in the shins, physically impossible only because he and his manager were both standing up.

"It's nice to have you here," said Pa to Valentino.

"I am grateful to be here," said Valentino. "I have often wanted to come, but I was told it was difficult to get a table unless you were known."

Father gave him the old eagle look, the raking glance, and then smiled. He had recognized something he liked —a genuinely modest statement from a truly modest man. He waved Valentino and his manager back to their seats, sat down with us, and signalled a bus boy to bring him a glass of ice water. From Father, this was the accolade; it meant that he was going to stay at your table for a while.

Two years later, at Sag Harbor, I drove into town for the evening papers and the headlines were about Valentino's death.

"Oh, no!" Father said, when I gave him the papers. "He was such a *nice* young man!"

Those nine words from Father always seemed to me a truer tribute than any expressed by the hysterical strangers who threw themselves upon Valentino's coffin at his famous funeral. Valentino was, indeed, "a nice young man."

Of all the famous people I came to know, partly through *Vanity Fair* but mainly through Father, Joseph

Hergesheimer became my greatest friend. Joe's friendship with Father had begun on the rainy night, already recounted in print, when Joe arrived at the Algonquin, a stranger, and found it full up, with no room available. He asked to speak to the proprietor and Father came on the telephone from his apartment.

"My name is Joseph Hergesheimer, and I find there is no room at the inn——" Joe began.

"Did you write a book called 'Java Head'?" Father demanded crisply.

"Yes," said Mr. Hergesheimer.

"You can have *my* room!" said Father.

Our own amity began one evening some time later when Joe, sitting in the Algonquin lobby with the family after dinner, asked me how old I was and how much I weighed. He was writing "*Linda Condon,*" the story of a hotel child, and statistics interested him.

"I'm twenty-one, and I weigh a hundred and twenty-one," I told him.

Joe leaned back, closed his eyes, and recited, " 'When I was a hundred and twenty-one. . . .' "

" 'I heard a wise man say. . . .' " I supplied automatically.

" 'Give crowns and pounds and guineas. . . .' " said Joe.

"But not your *weight* away!" I finished, oh so smartly.

Joe opened his eyes and looked at Father. "*This* girl has read a *book,*" he said.

The next day I ran into Mr. Hergesheimer on Forty-fourth Street outside the Algonquin, and he said many interesting things unfortunately unheard by me because of the noise made by the Sixth Avenue Elevated trains nearby. The El was undergoing a new paint job, and all of its cars wore a base-coat of bright orange.

"Goddamit!" said Joe finally. "Why does that El have to make more noise than *usual* today?"

"Probably because it's painted orange," I said, thinking it over, and with that simple remark Joe Hergesheimer and I became fast friends forevermore. You know how it is . . . somebody suddenly says something, and a spark lights up and kindles a lifetime devotion. I had the same thing happen to me the other day. A longtime acquaintance of mine named Alice Byrne was talking about her new beau. "He's not very handsome," she admitted to me, "in fact, I sometimes look at him and wonder why I bother with that fat old, bald thing. But then," Alice added, "I look in the mirror, and all of a sudden I say to myself, 'Oh Alice, you lucky, *lucky* girl!' "

Alice and I are friends forevermore, if she'll have me.

Joe Hergesheimer and his wife, Dorothy, often asked me to Dower House in West Chester, Pennsylvania, where they lived, and weekends there were romantic and stimulating. There was Joe, always managing to look rumpled in his fine English tweeds and Charvet linen, and there was Dorothy, cool, crisp and serene. There was the smell of grass and roses, and the feel of dew when you brushed against a hedge in the early evening. There were also distinguished guests, and I didn't always come off so well in that department. One weekend I told James Branch Cabell that I had enjoyed "*Jurgen,*" and he said, "Don't be a fool! You couldn't have enjoyed it at your age. Read it again when you're thirty." Another weekend, I shared a bathroom with Hugh Walpole and there was a hell of a row Sunday morning when Mr. Walpole couldn't find his toothbrush and accused me of stealing it. This accusation drove me to open warfare.

"What on earth would I want with your toothbrush?" I demanded of Mr. Walpole.

"You Ameddicans have done worse than that," the celebrated author informed me stormily. "My 'fans,' as you call them, would take the very fillings out of my *teeth* if they could get at them!"

I maintained a courteous silence, but the thought crossed my mind that Mr. Walpole would do better to keep his teeth in his mouth where they were safer.

It took all of Dorothy's charm and Joe's humor to make breakfast a pleasant occasion that morning, and they were not helped by Mr. Walpole who studied a timetable throughout the meal. He had a lecture engagement in New York that night, and was not convinced by reassurements from Dorothy and Joe that trains left nearby Philadelphia every hour on the hour.

"There seems to be a three-o'clock which will get me to New York at five," Mr. Walpole brooded aloud. "On the other hand, there is the two-o'clock, arriving at four, which would give me time to rest, bathe, and change before my lecture. But wait . . . there seems to be a faster train here . . . let me see. Yes, the four-o'clock which arrives at New York at five fifty-eight. Yes, that does it! The four-o'clock! Could your man drive me to the station for that one, Dorothy? If, of course, Miss Case is taking the same train, because it would be a pity for him to make the trip twice and I could easily take a *different* train if more convenient. What train *are* you taking, Miss Case?"

"Oh, I don't know," I moaned quietly into my coffee cup. "Couldn't we just . . . *leave?*"

I don't remember how, or when, we departed, but I do recall that I didn't take the same train as Mr. Walpole—to his rather obvious relief.

I wasn't truly as brash or precocious in my early twenties as the foregoing paragraphs might suggest. Actually, like most well-brought-up girls in the nineteen-twenties, I was extremely simple. I did my work at *Vanity Fair* satisfactorily enough to hold the job, but at home and out of office hours I moved in a kind of benign haze, sparked only by the fact that I was continually surrounded by bright people. Away from the Algonk—on a farm, or in a Midwestern town—I might have been considered plain stoopid. I read a lot, to be sure, but sometimes I chose books for peculiar reasons.

One evening Carl Van Vechten stopped me in the Algonquin lobby. I was wearing a brown velvet dress and carrying a book, as usual.

"What are you reading, Margaret?" Carl asked. He was a great friend of the family's and took a benevolent interest in me.

"Oh, I'm not reading it," I said, holding out the book. "It's just a book to carry with a dress."

This struck Carl so forcibly, though whether with horror or amusement I cannot say, that he immediately sent me a copy of his "Peter Whiffle," tastefully bound in brown and white and inscribed:

"For the supernal Margaret Case, this belated copy of 'Peter Whiffle,' to carry with a dress. From her admiring friend, Carl Van Vechten."

Possibly in an effort to wake me from my walking dream, Carl took me, in 1924, to the famous concert at which Paul Whiteman introduced Gershwin's *Rhapsody in*

Blue. Afterward Carl and his wife, Fania Marinoff, took me back to their apartment where Gershwin played the piano some more. All I remember of that historic evening is that I was seized with shyness and did not utter a word. In view of what Gershwin was soon to mean to music everywhere, I guess the shyness was not inappropriate.

I had asked Joe Hergesheimer to do some pieces for *Vanity Fair,* and he agreed to write a series to be called "Notebooks on Charm." This was a considerable favor to Crowny and me, since he was than at the height of his fame as a novelist and commanding vast sums from the *Saturday Evening Post.* When I wired him reminding him of this commitment and also stating the comparatively minute price *Vanity Fair* was able to pay him, Joe replied with the following telegram which I cherish:

> DEAR MARGARET TO WHOM COULD ANY NOTEBOOKS ON CHARM GO BUT TO YOU STOP AT THE SAME TIME I WAS DISMAYED BY THE COMPLETELY MERCENARY COLOR OF YOUR TELEGRAM STOP IT HAS SENT ME IMMEDIATELY OFF TO NEWPORT IN SEARCH OF THE WARM SYMPATHY AND SENSITIVE UNDERSTANDING THOSE ROCKS ARE CELEBRATED FOR STOP AND WITH LOVE.

Joe was a generous and entertaining letter writer. His letters were usually in longhand, on blue Dower House notepaper, and always signed (with a view to posterity) by his full name. Once, from Richmond where he had gone with Carl Van Vechten to visit Emily Clark and James Branch Cabell, he wrote:

> Dear Margaret,
>   Sunday turned into a sort of inferno of endless country lanes that were continually ending; I couldn't

find anything, not a road nor a signboard; and when, finally, the day slipped into dusk, and I realized what was happening to me, I got into a furious temper and from all the railroad stations I passed I telephoned passionately to everyone, as though I were lost on a derelict and sending up signals into the impersonal and unanswering night. You see, it had been planned very differently, with a long and tranquil ride to North Philadelphia and then a neat swing to where Mrs. Trigg was staying; but instead, I never, that time, saw you again, and only heard your voice echoing from that warm world that I had seemed to have lost forever. Well, against my intention, I came to Richmond with Carl and Mrs. Trigg on Tuesday; we got here at dinner time, I had something to eat quite by myself and then went at once to bed . . . where I stayed for eleven (11) hours. Carl had lunch today with Emily Clark; again I stayed in my room, with a gin fizz, and this afternoon we are going to the Cabells' for tea. . . . I am not working today, as you will have observed, nor tomorrow, and perhaps not the next day —I seem to have fallen into a need for solitude—but then I'll begin the documentation of Bale Hundred. . . . There is sun streaming in at the window, a gaunt wind, and the gin fizz is all gone. And soon I will be at a tea. Well, dear Margaret! It seems that I have no talent for writing, and that must come through the words that must come up. But meanwhile, I hope you liked it at Dower House. . . . You will, of course, come back—soon, and for the week spoken of, and whenever you can come I'll give Crowninshield a paper—on charm. . . . I have a wretched cold and more than a degree of fever. . . . Above the desk in this room there is an engraving called Daphnis and Chloë, and I envy them tremendously. It seems to be a pastoral affair with flowers and no thought of colds

—although it is a Victorian engraving—and I, in this connection, glanced into the mirror, and what I saw there—but about that you, at least, know the worst. Faithfully,

Joseph Hergesheimer

Enclosed in the letter was a clipping from a Richmond paper purporting to examine the sensations of Mr. James Branch Cabell at the thought of having five of America's leading novelists—Ellen Glasgow, Elinor Wylie, Joseph Hergesheimer, Carl Van Vechten and, of course, Cabell himself—convened in Richmond all at the same time. "Four of them," the article mused, "coming over a dark road to his house in one automobile.

"Who could have resisted?" the author concluded. "Mr. Cabell placed a log across the road, that ere morning America should have but one leading novelist."

Some of Joe's other letters were frivolous, especially when he was within sight of finishing a book. One began:

Do not live on capers,
Don't subsist on sauce:
One will give you vapors,
The other make you cross.

(And continued):
Saturday with luck, Balisand will be done. 96 thousand words . . . 36 days!
After Saturday, soon after, the paper on charm. . . .

The rum put in his tea
Was what affected he.

Love,
Joseph Hergesheimer
at Balisand in February,
1800.

I walked the half block from *Vanity Fair* to the Algonk every day for lunch—sometimes with old Gardner School friends like Marjorie Stralem or Polly Pollock or the Lovejoys, sometimes with Jeanne Ballot or Lois Long from the office, sometimes with the college beau of the moment. Lunch at the Algonquin, especially on the day after a play had opened, was as exciting as the theatre had been the night before. The star of the show was sure to be there, whether the play had been a success or a flop. If it was a hit, the star wished to receive the congratulations of friends and colleagues; if it was a failure he, or she, was in need of condolence and kind companions to point out that the acting had been flawless, but that the direction (or the script, or the sets, or the costumes, or the lighting) *stank*. A flop, among the tactful coterie of the Algonk, was always the fault of everybody involved except the person you were talking to.

On a typical day, Clifton Webb raced lightly through the lobby like a whippet nosing the wind—to lunch, perhaps, with Ina Claire, all chic and charm. Humphrey Bogart strode in, walking like a gunman after his first big hit as the gangster in *The Petrified Forest*. Over at the Round Table Robert Sherwood, the play's author, drooped amiably over his blue plate in the company of the rest of the Vicious Circle—Kaufman, Connelly, Adams, Benchley, Woollcott, Broun and Dorothy Parker. Jack Whiting, who had recently married Beth Fairbanks and won his first stage success in *America's Sweetheart* with Harriet Lake (now Ann Sothern), walked fast like a dancer through the luncheon crowd, beaming at everybody and curiously resembling Doug Fairbanks himself. And Helen Ford and Peggy Wood, co-starring in *Champagne Sec*, came in separately; Helen to meet some captivated swain or other in a flash of dimples, or possibly to lunch with Alex Clark and me; Peggy, as a rule, making more gravely toward the Round Table. It's odd that, although so many millions of television viewers now know Peggy Wood chiefly as "Mama," I remember "Mama" best as the singing star of *Maytime*, the operetta in which she introduced the lovely waltz that begins: "Sweetheart, sweetheart, sweetheart . . . Will you love me ever? . . ."

Mainly through Constance Collier, who had stayed at the Algonquin ever since she first came from England to play opposite William Gillette, the Algonk drew most of the English actors who converged upon New York in the 'twenties. Noel Coward was often there for lunch or dinner, although he usually rented a flat to live in because, by his own account, he likes to cook his own meals in the nude in warm weather and the Algonquin has no housekeeping apartments for naked people. Leslie Banks and Nigel Bruce both settled down there happily for the long run of *Springtime for Henry*, and Leslie Howard was, of course, an old friend. "I sometimes think," Father once said affectionately, "that the reason women are so crazy about Leslie is that he always looks as though he'd like to climb into their laps and have a good cry." Herbert Marshall and Edna Best, then married, stayed at the Algonk, and so did Colin Clive, Roy Royston, Joyce Barbour and Richard Bird, who was a remarkable Marchbanks opposite Katharine Cornell's "Candida." Gertrude Lawrence, Beatrice Lillie and Jack Buchanan were often among those present after the first *Charlot's Revue* opened. And I have mentioned in an earlier chapter those two delightfully British lobster-fanciers, Kenneth Douglas and Barry Baxter.

There was a trace of feeling among American actors

against the Englishmen coming over and, so to speak, taking the bread out of American mouths, but nobody could help admiring the British on a stage or liking them personally. Father loved them, even though I am certain he made little money from them, at lunchtime anyway. An English actor's favorite lunch is a dozen oysters and a bottle of Bass. It's one of my favorites, too.

Through the happy throng in the lobby and restaurant, Father strolled as serenely as though he had nothing on his mind beyond a chatty visit with his favorite friends. All sorts of crises might be threatening in the boiler room, on the roof, or anywhere between, but for a magic hour or two at lunchtime every day Father was able to forget them. His mingling with the patrons, listening to a story here, telling one there, was, of course, a part of his job and contributed largely to the famous "atmosphere" of the Algonquin; but, to Father, it was never anything but a pure delight.

Starting at the Algonk as night clerk, renting agent and general whipping boy, he had, for the past twenty years, owned the hotel's lease, equipment and business; but the building and the land it stood on was owned by an old New York family—or rather, by its last surviving member, an elderly lady who lived at the hotel. In 1927, Father bought the building and the land as well, and became sole owner, to the accompaniment of Horatio Alger-like headlines in the newspapers telling how a former humble employee had paid a million dollars for the Algonquin. Although this was a slight exaggeration, and Father deprecated it becomingly, I think he rather enjoyed the headlines; certainly he deserved them.

Complete ownership naturally brought him added responsibilities; but even in later, and sterner, years, when the depression and the unions both bared their fangs at him, the company of actors and writers always restored him. For many years the Algonquin employees had never been unionized, nor had they cared to be; they were well paid and happy in their jobs, and they liked and respected Father. Eventually, however, the unions won out (by a margin of one vote) and, although Father regretted the old person-to-person relationships, he was heard to mourn their loss aloud only once. He was sitting with Enid Markey and Ellis Baker at a table in the Rose Room one day when a thunderous crash from the kitchen proclaimed that some luckless bus boy had dropped a loaded tray. Father sighed.

"There was a time," he said to the girls, "when I would have gone out there and fired the man who did that. Now, I have to go out and say, 'Did you hurt yourself?'"

* Chapter 6 *

LIFE on *Vanity Fair* was as smooth and chic as a Noel
Coward drawing-room comedy, and with its own
undercurrents of passion. If it had ever been written as a play, it could have been called *Anna Karenina on
the Riviera*, or *A Streetcar Named the Ritz*. *Vogue*, another
Condé Nast publication with offices across the hall, had
many lady editors twinklingly receptive to dinner dates or
possibly, in one or two instances, matrimony with our
dashing publisher, Condé Nast; *Vanity Fair's* own managing
editor (whoever he happened to be) was usually wildly in
love with some feminine co-worker or contributor; almost
every editor wanted some other editor's secretary, strictly
for business purposes, of course; and such ceaseless warfare
went on among the editorial, advertising and art departments that we once, in later years, had to publish an apologetic letter to the hat manufacturers of America because
I had printed a full-page picture of Douglas Fairbanks Jr.,
hatless, remarking in the caption that he never wore a hat
and didn't own one. This, the hatters claimed, was enough
to start a fashion trend among young men that could put
them out of business.

Through all the controlled agitation Frank Crownin-shield, our editor, moved like an April breeze. Pink-cheeked, white-haired and crisply tailored, Crowny walked lightly with his toes pointed out and with an air of constantly being about to bow to somebody. "Hello, boy," he would say, blithely passing a male acquaintance on his way to the main event which was always, for Crowny, the seemingly unexpected, delightful discovery of a beautiful woman in his path. Crowny loved the company of good-looking women and was ever their faithful squire, but he was a confirmed bachelor and lived in a Park Avenue penthouse with Condé Nast, who was also a bachelor but less confirmed than Crowny, being at the time "between" his two marriages.

Frank Crowninshield *was Vanity Fair*, just as Frank Case was the Algonquin. He was the magazine's editor for twenty-two years, from 1914 until it merged with *Vogue* in 1936, and he spent a large part of that time engaged in a valiant struggle with Condé Nast over the merits of modern art. It was not, in fact, until the last fifteen years of *Vanity Fair's* individual existence that Crowny won Nast over to the idea of publishing full-page reproductions in color of the works of Modigliani, Matisse, Picasso, Braque and his other idols.

Crowninshield was born in Paris in 1872, the son of Frederic Crowninshield, a Boston painter with an independent income, and grew up in France, Italy and Boston. His family connections were both impeccable and colorful, a cousin of his father's having married John Quincy Adams II and another, earlier, forebear having been hanged for piracy. At the age of eighteen, Frank came to New York and went to work in Putnam's Bookstore for eight dollars a week (he was raised to ten dollars the following year), and in 1895 became publisher of the *Bookman* for Dodd Mead & Company. At this time he also began to write humorous and satirical pieces under the pen name of Arthur Loring Bruce. Between 1900 and 1914 he was assistant editor of *Munsey's* and art editor of *Century* and, always a sociable fellow, had become a member of the Knickerbocker Club and had begun to circulate at dinners and other parties where he met another, equally gregarious, young man about town, Condé Nast.

In 1913, Nast, who had been publishing *Vogue* for four years, bought from Doubleday Page a fashion magazine called *Dress*, because he thought it might be a possible rival to *Vogue*. He also paid three thousand dollars for the name of a defunct publication called *Vanity Fair*, and published the combined magazines under the title, *Dress and Vanity Fair*. He was not satisfied with the magazine, however, and in time consulted Crowninshield about it. Crowninshield suggested that the new periodical should cover "the things people talk about—parties, the arts, theatre, sports, humor and so on," and that it should leave the affairs of *haute couture* to *Vogue*. Nast asked him to become its editor, and Crowninshield dropped the fashion drawings and the name *Dress*, and started it on its way as *Vanity Fair*.

Although its circulation never rose above ninety thousand, *Vanity Fair* was for many years unique among magazines. It typified the chic world, the world of taste, elegance and leisure, and it was openly addressed to readers who had time for all of those things. Furthermore, as time went on, its printing, format, photography and color reproductions became the handsomest of any publication's. As a magazine it reflected both the fastidious and the sociable qualities of its publisher and its editor—two men who had much in common, although for a time it was popular to speak of Nast as the hardheaded business man and Crowninshield as the dreamer. That Crowninshield, an eighth-generation New England Yankee, was no dreamer, was proved in 1929 when other men, including Nast, were all but wiped out by the stock-market crash. Crowninshield had put all of *his* money into a collection of modern paintings, sculptures, drawings, lithographs and illustrated books. In 1943, five years before his death, he sold a large part of his collection at auction, in order to simplify things for his executors. It brought one hundred and eighty thousand dollars.

Crowny, the born clubman, helped to found the Cavendish Club (a gathering of bridge players) and the Atlantic Beach, Coffee House, Dutch Treat, and West Side Tennis Clubs. He was also one of the seven founders of the Museum of Modern Art. He knew so many people, and was in such demand as toastmaster at dinners that someone once said, "Frank Crowninshield has introduced everybody who has ever *been* introduced, and in most cases he introduced them to each other." His friends ranged from the dowager Mrs. Vanderbilt to Gypsy Rose Lee, from Aldous Huxley to Houdini. Although a great one for proposing toasts, he never in his life tasted alcohol, and he attributed this to an incident in his childhood. It seems his grandmother had taken him, at the age of ten, to a temperance meeting in Boston where the speaker urged all those who wished to take the teetotal pledge to stand up. Several ladies stood up, including Frank's grandmother, and Frank, who had been brought up never to sit in the presence of standing ladies, also got politely to his feet. He swore off smoking somewhere around the turn of the century, after an all-night poker game in a smoky room in the company of Will

Irwin, Rupert Hughes and Charles Hanson Towne. From that time he was eloquent against the evils of tobacco, and was forever offering some lost cigarette fiend one of the square white peppermint tablets he himself habitually used.

Crowny was a kind of unsung arbiter of the guest lists for Condé Nast's famous parties at his penthouse. These lists, which themselves became famous in a secret sort of way, were at first graded A, B and C, according to the guest's social standing; but as high society and the arts began to intermingle and merge (and Nast, under Crowny's urging, was largely credited with the change), the lists came to be headed:

> Married People—Society
> Single People —Society
> Married People—Theatre
> Single People —Theatre
> Married People—Other Arts
> Single People —Other Arts.

Those were wonderful parties. I remember one in particular, not only because it was the first time I had too much champagne (not being used to any) but because, feeling wretched and dizzy, I looked around frantically for some trusted friend to take me quietly home. Guess whom I picked as the trusted friend? None other than that trenchant boulevardier, Clifton Webb. And Mother Machree in person could not have been more solicitous than he. He got my wrap from the cloakroom, and whisked me tenderly into a cab and home to the Algonquin with only one stop on the way, at a Childs' where he fed me a "prairie oyster"—also my first and, I devoutly hope, my last.

I don't remember ever seeing Crowny dance at the parties,

but his tact and charm made the ladies love him, not only at parties but at the office, and even when he was rejecting their contributions to *Vanity Fair*. To watch Crowny turn down a would-be contributor was an education for any young editor. One time a lady artist who specialized in drawing cats came in with a portfolio of sketches, of cats only, and Crowny looked through them carefully, emitting small cries of admiration while the artist glowed hopefully at his side.

"These are truly little masterpieces!" he exclaimed. Closing the portfolio, he took off his pince-nez and leaned back thoughtfully. "Unfortunately, my dear," he added, "we can't use any drawings of cats at the moment." The artist drooped. "But I'll tell you what you do," said Crowny (the artist brightened again); "you go home and draw a whole lot of *dogs*, hundreds and hundreds of all kinds of dogs, Pekes, Chihuahuas, Labrador retrievers and so on, and then we'll see! Thank you *so* much, dear, it was a pleasure. Good-bye."

He might as well have told her to go home and draw a floor plan of the Manhattan sewerage system, and he knew it; she was strictly a cat artist. We saw her no more, but I subsequently learned that she always maintained, throughout her career, that Frank Crowninshield was the most charming and most encouraging editor she had ever met.

Crowny's suggestions to authors were equally kind, fluent, and generally just as impossible. To a writer who lamented that he couldn't seem to think up a plot, Crowny would respond sympathetically, "Nonsense, dear boy. There is this bronze idol in a Chinese temple, you see, with an emerald in its forehead, and you have sworn to steal this emerald and bring it to this girl whom you are in love with, because her father is an archeologist . . ." Or, "Plot?" he would say. "Dear boy, there are plots everywhere you look. For instance, you see this African mask on my desk? Well, this girl whom you are in love with wakes up one morning and finds this mask on her pillow as a sort of threat from a gang of international thieves who plan to kidnap her because her father is the head of Scotland Yard. . . ." Usually the author would thank him with feeling, and go away moaning.

Crowny's relations with his writers were, on the whole, affectionate but shrewd. When I was at *Vanity Fair*, and after it had moved from 19 West Forty-fourth Street to the Graybar Building on Lexington Avenue, we had weekly office luncheons in a private room, with eggs Benedict (a favorite dish of Crowny's) sent up from the Savarin Restaurant and, as guest of honor, some celebrated author whom Crowny was anxious to entrap, such as André Maurois, Michael Arlen, or Thomas Wolfe. Conversationally, Crowny was at his most brilliant during these gatherings, giving off little anecdotes about the dinner party the night before at Mrs. Vanderbilt's, or the ball at Mrs. Twombly's the night before that. Nearly always the celebrated author was so dazzled by these glimpses into high life that he found himself agreeing to work for *Vanity Fair* at a lower rate that he had planned.

Jeanne Ballot, a Parisian-looking girl with the down-to-earth mental approach of the born Brooklynite she was, was Crowny's secretary for over twenty-five years, until his death, and he would regularly abandon the Vanderbilt and Twombly tables to dine with Jeanne and her parents in Brooklyn—an outing which always gave him extreme pleasure. Jeanne knew him perhaps better than anyone did, and had ceased to be startled by him, but he sometimes faintly alarmed the newer secretaries and stenographers by the warmth of his genuine interest in them. Proceeding by his own premise that any young girl must, perforce, be in love, he gave them endless fatherly advice on love affairs which were often purely nonexistent. "You think you love him *now*," he would say, pausing by some stenographer's desk, "but think of the years ahead!" And he would pass on lightly.

Once, engaging a new girl as assistant to Jeanne, he brought forth from a desk drawer some photographs of the Denishawn Dancers, lightly draped, performing rhythmically upon the sward in Central Park. "These," he said, "are some of my former secretaries, and what we used to do on Saturday afternoons." Another time, when a new secretary came to work with him at home, where he was confined with grippe, he handed her a small painting of a reclining nude. "One of my former secretaries," he informed her. "Terribly capable girl. I hope you will do as well."

Once over their first fright, these girls, like all the other office workers, came to adore Crowny. They knew that his interest in them was as practical as it was dreamy. One day, with the magazine going to press, Crowny was missing from his office and home, and the presses had to be held up for three hours while everybody frantically searched for him. "Do you know where we finally located him?" Condé Nast later raged. "At the funeral of some messenger-girl's mother!"

It was not in Crowny to be unkind, or even brusque, to anyone. If he couldn't gracefully get rid of a pest any other way, he did it by giving him an enthusiastic letter of introduction to someone else. Such letters flowed so freely from him that they became more of a liability than an asset to any applicant, since the recipient's reaction to yet one more of Crowny's rosy recommendations was usually an instantaneous "Throw the bum out!" However, even the victims of his kindness—the busy men who were constantly faced with his earnest recommendations of people he couldn't otherwise shake off—enjoyed his letters. They were gay, warm, amusing, and almost always signed, "Ever thine." I wish I had saved all the letters and notes I had from Crowny; I can find only one, written in 1925 when I had taken a leave of absence from *Vanity Fair* to get married and go on a honeymoon to Havana. (I don't remember what the "manilla wrapper" was; surely nothing concerned with cigars, since Crowny didn't smoke, and I don't *think* I brought him a dressing gown from Cuba. Probably some forgotten intramural joke.)

Dear Margaret (Crowny wrote in his usual spidery hand on his usual Knickerbocker Club notepaper)

You were so sweet and kind to bring me that wonderful present, and I can hardly thank you enough for it, and for the gift, too, of your friendship—an even more sumptuous gift than that enchanting manilla wrapper. The latter will serve to keep me warm— when you have withdrawn from me the final semblance of amity—a prospect which (even if not imminent) I can hardly face with fortitude or equanimity. I have thought so often of you, dear, and have missed incessantly your coarse and meaningless features in my *bureau de travail*.

How fortunate for you that Destiny, having denied you the gifts of Beauty and Personal Allure, should have bestowed upon you the comfort invariably following in the train of homely honesty and rude health.

When shall I see you, dear friend! There is no one, I have learned, quite like you.

Heaps of affection to you, from

Uncle Frank

It interests me to compare Crowny's letter with one I received, some years later, from my next boss, Harold Ross of *The New Yorker*. Ross's letter was also a kind of thank-you note, written at a time when, having sold a few Profiles to *The New Yorker*, I was suddenly in demand and was writing for national magazines like *Good Housekeeping* and *The Saturday Evening Post* for twice my *New Yorker* pay. My heart was still with *The New Yorker*, and there must have been some correspondence about it, because Ross's letter (again the only one I seem to have saved) reads as follows, in Ross's own jumpy typing and all in one paragraph:

Dear Margaret:

Thanks for *your* wonderful letter. Since you love to work for us so much, you just go ahead and do it. Your New Yorker output has irked me for a long time by its insufficiency. I'm always depressed by the appearance of your pieces elsewhere, and the strange expeditions you are reported to make. For instance, what in God's name were you doing in the Hotel Mayflower, 50 rooms, European plan, Fireproof, Ralph G. Lorenz, manager, Plymouth, Mich.? Don't answer; regard the question as rhetorical. It's all too sordid, probably. Shawn has arranged to pay you a little more and maybe that will have its effect. I hope it will. I hope there will be many pieces from you right away.

Sincerely,

Ross

So there you have two editors, one devious and one direct. Crowny was a man who patted your hand, and Ross was a man who called it. Both, to my mind, were great editors.

When I first went to work at *Vanity Fair*, at twenty-five dollars a week, I was given a desk in John McMullin's office, a windowless cubicle adjoining Crowny's large, well-lighted suite. Mr. McMullin, who wrote men's fashions under the pseudonym of "Him," regarded my intrusion with what I can only describe as a matronly indignation. He had his desk moved so that his back was to me, and I came to know the back of the McMullin head with its upsweep to hide the bald spot better than I knew the back of my own. Perhaps that was why I enjoyed opening the door to Crowny's office where the sun streamed in, and perhaps that is why I shall never forget one particular day when I opened Crowny's door.

I had learned to wear a hat in the office, like the *Vogue* ladies across the hall, and on this day I was wearing a new white felt number, wide-brimmed and trimmed with crimson poppies around the crown. I wasn't thinking of the hat, however, when I beheld the scene before me as I opened Crowny's door. In a shaft of sunlight stood the most beautiful young man I had ever seen. The sunbeam illumined his blond hair, and the eyes he turned on me were bluer than aquamarines. The same sunbeam apparently lit up my white hat and the interested face under it because, in the split second before I closed the door, I heard the young man say, "Hey! Who was *that?*"

Crowny called me back and introduced us. "Margaret," he said, "this is Scott Fitzgerald."

I have often wished that I could have known Scott Fitzgerald while the radiance was still on him. The next time I saw him, some ten years later, he was a tired old man. He had been living in Father's beach house at Malibu, which he had rented while he was trying to write a Hollywood movie, and coming East on some hopeless business or other, he took me out to dinner. He was drinking only beer, but in such quantities that it took all of his native good manners to conceal the burps. We went to a night club and Scott, beating time to the orchestra with his fist on the table and watching the people dancing, made his only coherent remark of the evening.

"You know something?" he said to me. "I *invented* this!"

He did, too.

The nineteen-twenties, when I first started to work for *Vanity Fair*, were exciting years for everybody in New York. In the single season of 1924, for example, the plays on Broadway included *What Price Glory?*, *Desire under the Elms*, *They Knew What They Wanted; Grounds for Divorce*, starring Ina Claire; *Candida*, starring Katharine Cornell; and a revival of *The Second Mrs. Tanqueray*, starring Ethel Barrymore; the musicals were also a rich assortment . . . *Charlot's Revue*, introducing Gertrude Lawrence, Beatrice Lillie and Jack Buchanan; the Marx Brothers in *I'll Say She Is;* Fred and Adele Astaire in *Lady Be Good*, Will Rogers and Ann Pennington in *The Ziegfeld Follies*, Dennis King and Mary Ellis in *Rose Marie;* Grace Moore,

Fannie Brice and Clark & McCullough in Irving Berlin's *Music Box Revue;* and Moran and Mack and the Dolly Sisters in *The Greenwich Village Follies.* The "pop" songs of that year, in addition to show tunes, were *Jealous, Amapola, California Here I come!, What'll I Do?,* and *The Man I Love.*

Pulitzer Prizes went to *The New York World* for journalism, to Sidney Howard's *They Knew What They Wanted* for drama, and to Edna Ferber's novel, "So Big." We were reading Sinclair Lewis's "Babbitt," Joseph Hergesheimer's "The Bright Shawl" and "Balisand," Scott Fitzgerald's "The Beautiful and Damned," Booth Tarkington's "Alice Adams," Hendrik Van Loon's "Story of Mankind," and Carl Van Vechten's "The Tattooed Countess." It was the year of the Teapot Dome oil scandals, the death of Lenin, and the Dawes Plan. All the girls wore their belts around their hips and their skirts to their knees, and I had my hair bobbed, which caused a momentary coolness between Father and Elsie Janis's mother when Mrs. Janis remarked, "I suppose it's very chic but frankly, dear, that flat back to your head makes your nose look much bigger." Father didn't like the bob either, but he wasn't going to let anyone *else* criticize it.

The bob was mainly Father's fault, anyway. Owing to the several thousand hairpins I was obliged to wear in my long hair to keep it up, I had become inclined to shed hairpins far and wide in odd places, and finally Father tacked a little note over the mirror in my bathroom. The note read as follows:

> Do not drop the hairpin down the little lou,
> You will need a plumber every time you do;
> Plumbers do not answer the cries of people who
> Drop the beastly hairpin down the little lou.

Working at *Vanity Fair* and going home to lunch every day at the Algonquin was as exhilarating as mountain air. The Algonquin Rose Room had entered upon such a glorious phase of its celebrity-packed career that the Shakespearean actor, Fritz Leiber, one day complained to Father about it. "The only trouble with this room, Frank," he said sadly, "is that there are too many Hamlets in it." Father followed this particular Hamlet's melancholy gaze to two nearby tables; at the first sat Walter Hampden, at the second John Barrymore.

The tempo of life in general encouraged hard work, and pretty soon I was promoted to an associate editorship with a raise in pay to forty dollars a week. In addition to assembling the theatre pages, I then interviewed authors, read manuscripts, translated articles and stories from the French, wrote a monthly short-short story of my own (one hundred dollars extra), ran an annual *Vanity Fair* beauty contest at Grand Central Palace for publicity purposes, and thought up and assembled dozens of "trick" pages such as a page of photographs of the backs of famous heads (Guess Who This Is?) and a page of Daily Doubles— pictures of obscure people who were the spittin' image of famous people. Since *Vanity Fair* was already beginning to be accused, in some quarters, of being too "arty," I tried to inject the popular note by getting Doug Fairbanks Jr., to write a series of biographical sketches of Hollywood stars illustrated by his own caricatures (they were surprisingly good, too), and by engaging that somewhat earthier artist, Milt Gross of "Nize Baby" fame, to do a series of cartoons for us.

Only one of my innovations could be called permanent. One day Carl Van Vechten sent me a young painter armed with a note from Carl and a portfolio full of drawings.

I knew nothing about painting but I liked what I saw, and—contrary to rules—I took the youth and his work immediately into Crowny's office. Crowny bought two *Vanity Fair* covers from him on the spot, and Miguel Covarrubias is still kind enough to say that this was the start of his American career.

I was just as good at mistakes as I was at innovations. One of my biggest goofs concerned a page we ran opposite the well-known "We Nominate for the Hall of Fame" which was called "We Nominate for the Hall of Oblivion." I enjoyed suggesting names for Oblivion, and I never felt a creamier satisfaction than when I nominated, and saw published, a picture of Bernarr Macfadden on this page. To me, Bernarr Macfadden was not only a frustrated murderer who incited nice old men to drop dead by making them do push-ups, he also published distressing magazines called *True Romance*, *Love and Romances*, *Dream World*, and so on. I considered that the world could do without him. How could I know that this Macfadden would be parachuting from an airplane twenty-nine years later, on practically the same day that I became a grandmother?

The issue of *Vanity Fair* that interred Bernarr Macfadden sold out rapidly on the newsstands and gave us quite a flood of comment in newspaper columns. I sat back and received the congratulations of my colleagues, and waited for the final accolade from Condé Nast. Condé was away at the time, up in Greenwich where he had established the Condé Nast Press which now prints not only the Nast magazines but many others, including *The New Yorker*. At the time, it was a new project and took a good deal of Condé's time.

A day or so later, however, I heard his light, fast-stepping approach along the corridor, and he appeared before my desk.

"How are you, Margaret?" he inquired, and then just as smoothly, "Whose idea was it to put Bernarr Macfadden in the Hall of Oblivion?"

"It was *mine!*" I beamed.

"Well," said Condé, "that picture cost me exactly fifty thousand dollars. Bernarr Macfadden was ready to sign a fifty-thousand-dollar contract with the Condé Nast Press to print *Dance Magazine* when he happened to pick up a copy of this month's *Vanity Fair*. The deal, dear Margaret, is *off!*"

I will never know why Condé didn't fire me for that costly inspiration. He didn't fire me, but from that time on all *Vanity Fair* editors were required to submit to Mr. Nast their nominees for Oblivion before the page went through for publication. With that kind of censorship, sensible though it was, the Oblivion page soon lost its spirit and disappeared.

The "Oblivion" page was actually the idea of a beautiful blonde named Clare Boothe Brokaw, who had travelled purposefully across the hall from *Vogue* to work at *Vanity Fair*. Clare and I shared a large, sunny office adjoining that of our managing editor, Donald Freeman, which in turn adjoined Crowny's silver-papered chamber. Clare, like the princesses in the fairy stories, was not only beautiful but good, and the first time I had an inkling of the firmness under the façade was when I came to work one morning and found that she was employing my secretary and I was employing hers. It seems that Clare preferred my secretary, and had engaged her by the simple means of paying her twice her usual salary out of her own pocket, or rather out of the ample alimony bestowed by Mr. George Brokaw.

I didn't mind much. One secretary was as good as another, to me, and after all, I only wanted my job; I didn't want to be President of the Condé Nast Publications, as it became increasingly evident that Clare did. Condé later told me with a nervous chuckle that Clare, only a few months after she went to work on *Vanity Fair*, came to him and offered to buy a controlling interest in Condé Nast Publications. Condé didn't sell.

It would be ridiculous to criticize or mock any woman as obviously able and successful as Clare Boothe Luce, our present ambassador to Italy. Besides, I liked Clare very much and we got along famously together at *Vanity Fair*, as soon as I realized that, when Clare wanted something, no mere human being must stand in the way. For example, there was the affair of the first-night tickets.

As drama editor I received first-night tickets to all the new plays. One morning, on the day of a big opening, I left my tickets on my desk while I went out to lunch, and when I looked for them around five-thirty they were gone. After a frantic and vain search, I called up the press agent who agreed to have duplicates for me at the box office that night.

When my date and I walked down the theatre aisle with my duplicate tickets, guess who had the real tickets and was occupying my seats? Right. None other than Clare Boothe and escort. I was so mad that I merely said to her, "Enjoy the play, dear," and stalked back up the aisle. My date and I went to the movies.

Next morning in the office Clare said, "But you left the tickets on your desk, so of course I thought you didn't *want* them!"

I only hope she is as smart with those Eyetalians.

On the other hand, Clare could be a good companion

and even a good sport when it was necessary. I had spent many happy weekends with Joe and Dorothy Hergesheimer at Dower House in West Chester, Pennsylvania; I particularly remember one masquerade party at the Pickering Hunt Club where all of the older women wore daringly naked costumes and I, aged twenty-two, made a mild sensation by appearing covered from neck to ankle in the robes of an eighteenth-century French marquise. Joe and Dorothy, hearing of Clare's beauty and wit, asked me to bring her out for a weekend. "There'll be a party Saturday night," Joe said, and I swear that is *all* he said.

When we arrived Saturday noon, Dorothy said, "Where are your costumes for tonight? What are you kids going as?"

After a horrid silence we learned that the party was another fancy-dress party, and we were supposed to have brought costumes. Clare might very well have blamed me for not preparing her with the news, but apparently one look at my face convinced her that it was news to me as well. Joe hurried us into the village where we bought the only costumes we could find, a pair of blue denim overalls each, and that night Clare calmly and sweetly beat the former marquise at her own game.

I wore the overalls as they came, plunging neckline, bare arms and naked back and all. Clare filled in *her* overalls with the primmest, whitest, high-necked and long-sleeved blouse this side of a Quaker colony—and once again the covered girl was the cover-girl of the evening.

As a young woman who was practically never wrong, Clare had a sure-fire way of triumphing over her occasional defeats. The next day, Sunday, Joe and I went for a walk and came home to find Clare in the library, a book in one hand and a paper cutter in the other. She held them both out to us. "Joe!" she cried. "You have such wonderful books, and you don't even *read* them!" She had cut all the pages in an "uncut" edition, thereby reducing its value from some hundreds of dollars to nothing at all. Joe reeled only slightly, and was soon restored by Clare who, realizing her crime, began to bombard him with questions about it. That was the way she conquered her mistakes—by asking questions about them.

"*Why* mustn't the pages be cut, Joe?" she asked him. "What makes a book valuable with uncut pages, and worthless when the pages are cut? Please explain this to me, Joe, I want to *know* about it."

I left them in the library and joined Dorothy on the terrace.

There is a gal who is going to know everything about everything, sooner or later," I said.

"Yes," said Dorothy with her usual tranquillity. "Isn't it lovely out here?"

I have said that Clare was a good companion, and so she was. We had adjoining rooms at Dower House, and both nights of that weekend Clare barged into my room in her nightgown, flung herself across my bed, and started a real old-fashioned bull session. We giggled and laughed so much that Joe, clad in his Bond Street pajamas and Charvet dressing gown, came across the hall from his room to join the party. The curly-maple room (my regular guest room at Dower House) rocked with laughter those nights, and I sometimes think that they were the only times that Clare Boothe ever enjoyed a true, hilarious mirth with no special aim in view. Her laughter in later years always seemed to me to be deliberately spaced for effect, and therefore a little forced and more than a little hollow. It is the laughter of someone who insists that she has a sense of humor. I like to remember our ambassador to Italy as that nice girl who got the giggles over absolutely nothing, along with me, at Joe Hergesheimer's Dower House in West Chester, Pennsylvania.

Clare, no matter how giggly out of office hours, was the force that changed *Vanity Fair* from a magazine of style and entertainment into a political instrument, and thereby (I think) destroyed it. To be sure, she had Condé Nast on her side, although it was partly out of desperation. *Vanity Fair* had been losing money steadily since 1929, and Condé had strongly urged Crowny to run some pieces that would attract men readers as well as women. Crowny's attitude about this was (a) that women bought magazines, not men, and (b) that *Vanity Fair* was addressed to cultivated people of either sex, and that what a cultivated woman would read, a cultivated man would read, too. Later years, and other magazines, proved him shiningly right on his first premise. His second is still debatable, although he clung to his belief in cultivated people (of both sexes) and, even during World War II, was heard to remark that the "Allies" could not fail to win because Hitler and Mussolini were "boors," and Roosevelt and Churchill were "cultivated people."

When Nast and Clare Boothe descended on Crowny with the demand that he publish political articles in *Vanity Fair*, it was as though they had handed him a baseball bat and required him to beat to death the nearest small stenographer. He couldn't do it. He worried visibly, and one day he took me to lunch at the Crillon.

"What do you think of this idea of political articles, Margaret?" he asked me.

"I don't know," I told him. "I don't know a thing about

politics, and besides, I'm not allowed to see any of the articles until they're in final proof."

"You and I are in the same boat," sighed Crowny. And then he suddenly brightened, and said, "You and I, dear Margaret, have the quality *Vanity Fair* needs—the quality of *gaiety*. Let us strive to keep it in the magazine, shall we?"

We strove, Crowny and I, but Condé and Clare were too much for us. They had already engaged John Franklin Carter, an employee of the State Department, to write a series of articles under the pen-name of "Jay Franklin." As "Jay Franklin," Carter wrote a number of political articles for *Vanity Fair*, including one called "Wanted: A New Party," in which he called for something he named a "New Deal." Later, as a member of President Roosevelt's Brain Trust, Carter contributed this phrase to the President, so he must remain as an historical figure, although I don't know where he is now.

Clare accomplished even more, at *Vanity Fair*, than an occasional political article. She founded her own political party, in an office down the hall. It was called the New Nationalist Party, and its members included Mrs. Harrison Williams and Mrs. James Forrestal. Clare Boothe was, naturally, president.

The New Nationalist Party sent delegates to both sides of the Presidential campaign of 1932. Clare Boothe (then Mrs. Brokaw) appeared at the Democratic National Convention in Chicago, to try to win recruits to the New Nationalists. Mrs. Harrison Williams appealed to the Republicans at the same place, for the same reason. For some reason or other, both girls failed dismally . . . possibly because they were not campaigning for any president but for an ideal, a *new* deal. After all these years, you have to give them the benefit of the doubt.

Frank Crowninshield was one man who did not give Clare Boothe Brokaw or Mrs. Harrison Williams the benefit of any doubt. He thought they were crazy, and he told them so. "Dear girls," he said to them, "don't you know that the sight of a lovely woman shouting in public is unattractive to any man?" When they paid him no attention and set off for the convention anyway, Crowny made a mournful remark that has rung down the ages:

"The Number Two company of *Joan of Arc*" he explained; and added, "I presume that the girls have had their swords forged by Cartier."

The New Nationalist Party evaporated after its defeat at the convention, but Clare Boothe came back to *Vanity Fair* more than ever determined to make it an important political magazine. It was a tough time for Crowny. "Now they're even making me *read* these political articles!" he moaned to me once.

I tried to do something about it. I asked Condé to lunch with me one day at the Algonquin, and I told him plainly that *Vanity Fair* was losing its gaiety, that there were too many political articles in it. I remember his answer. He patted my hand, looked at me fondly, and said, "Margaret, you're only twenty-two, what do you know about politics?"

"That's just the point!" I shrieked. "I can't even READ *Vanity Fair* any more, let alone help edit it!"

"Look," said Condé, "I agree that the light, satirical side of *Vanity Fair* is important, and I rely on Crowny, with your help, to keep up that side. But there must also be an important side to the magazine, a heavier side, and I must

supply that with the help of Clare Boothe. Isn't that fair enough?"

I remember my answer, which was shrewd beyond my years. "Yes, of course, Condé," I said, "except—have you ever seen a seesaw with a heavy child on one end and a slim child on the other? The slim child hasn't got a chance."

"Oh, don't be precocious!" said Condé impatiently, and I knew it was no use talking to him any more.

I stayed on at *Vanity Fair*, watching the political pieces outnumber the humor and satire three to one, but I never saw the handwriting on the wall for me personally until the early 'thirties. At that time, Condé Nast engaged as art editor of Nast Publications a German-educated Turk named M. F. Agha, who revolutionized the graceful format of *Vanity Fair* into a series of modernistic squares with no capital letters anywhere. This new design soon became the means of almost obliterating me entirely. Having been married, divorced, and a mother by that time, I had retained my ex-husband's name and was in the habit of signing my monthly short story in *Vanity Fair* "Margaret Case Morgan." One day the proof pages of my piece came back to me for correction with the title reading as follows:

dude ascending a staircase
by
margaret case mor

I pencilled a large red question mark beside this hieroglyphic and returned it to Mr. Agha, who speedily sent it back to me again with this memo:

mrs. morgan:
    your name is too long. we cannot squeeze it in. it
ruins the looks of the whole page.

                                                    m.f. agha.

All of Crowny's charm was required to persuade Mr.
Agha to let me use my own name as a signature.

In spite of Agha's typographical tricks, and the insistence
of Condé and Clare on more and more political articles—
or perhaps because of those two things—*Vanity Fair* eventually lost the battle against changing times and particularly against a new magazine called *The New Yorker*. In
1936 *Vanity Fair* merged with *Vogue*, with Crowny becoming advisory editor to both publications; and gradually
the famous combination of Frank Crowninshield-and-
Vanity Fair disappeared, along with the gay and easy world
it had served for over twenty years to illustrate and enter-
tain.

* Chapter 7 *

MY own safe world of actors and writers, of the Algonquin and *Vanity Fair*, rocked slightly when, in the nineteen-twenties, I became engaged to marry Morgan Morgan, a stockbroker who, with his parents, tended to stiffen up in the presence of the lively arts. Morgan broke the news to me firmly during his courtship, when he criticized my choice of friends.

"No actress is decent," he proclaimed, "and all writers are bums."

I must have truly loved the guy, because I kept refusing the trip around the world Father anxiously kept offering, and I even listened to another little homily from Morgan, later on. He had asked me whether I planned to be married from the Algonquin, and I said yes, naturally. Morgan turned pale.

"It's just that the Algonquin is a *theatrical* hotel," he explained, "and you know how the family feels about *that*. Not that your father isn't a gentleman, of course—Dad says he seems to be a perfect gentleman. But, well . . ." Morgan concluded, "it isn't as though he were manager of the Ritz!"

I looked at him, bewildered. "You mean that if Father were manager of the Ritz, everything would be all right?"

"Of course," Morgan said simply.

This time the message got through, and seven generations of fighting Americans rose up in me.

"Listen," I said. "My father is no manager of any hotel, he owns his own hotel. It is a famous hotel, where illiterates like you are not tolerated. And furthermore, for your information," I intoned, "when my father walks into the Ritz, the manager of the Ritz KNEELS!"

I am sure that Mr. Albert Keller, who was then manager of the Ritz and a good friend of Father's, would have forgiven this exaggeration if he had heard it.

Father never heard about the manager-of-the-Ritz interlude, at least not from me, but he must have known I was disturbed because he said, one day, "How would you and Morgan like to be married from Elsie's house in Tarrytown? Elsie and Ma Janis have offered it."

I will never know how word of the difficulty between Morgan and me got to Father, or how Elsie and Mrs. Janis heard about it. I have sometimes thought, since then, of the pang it must have cost Father *not* to have me married from the Algonquin he was so proud of; and of the wonderfully good friends he had in Elsie and Mrs. Janis, who so quickly and quietly came to his rescue. It's a pity that it takes so many years to realize things like that.

The Janises gave Morgan and me a beautiful wedding at Philipse Manor and on that day, anyway, Father had the last word. It was a bitterly cold day in November and Morgan's father and mother arrived frozen, after the long drive from New York.

"I've got a chill, get me a drink," was Mr. Morgan Senior's first remark, to Elsie's butler who opened the door.

The butler bowed, went away, and returned with a message.

"I am sorry, sir," he told Mr. Morgan, "but Mr. Case says that there will be no drinking or carousing until after the ceremony."

When Morgan and I took off for a honeymoon in Havana, Father commissioned me to bring him back some of his favorite cigars. A few days later, to refresh my memory, I received the following cable:

MRS. MORGAN MORGAN
HAVANA-HAVANA
CUBA-CUBA
CORONA-CORONA
(signed) PAPA-PAPA

Morgan turned out to be pretty nice after I married him. Although Clarence Day had not yet written "Life with Father," Morgan embodied, at twenty-eight, every quality of Father Day; he was solid, dependable, kind, stubborn, a little smug, and determined at all cost to hide the fact that he had a heart of pure mush. I sometimes regret that I was too young and ignorant at the time to appreciate his qualities. Unfortunately my friends—those indecent actresses and those bums, the writers—didn't appreciate him any more than I did. They found him pompous, and blamed him unfairly for things he had not done. One night Elsie and Mrs. Janis came to dinner with us, when Elsie was playing at the Palace. After dinner (during which Mrs. Janis, to Morgan's distress, had fed her dessert to a rather soiled Pekinese in her lap), we repaired to the living room for coffee and liqueurs, and I happened to look at the clock. "Hey," I said to Elsie, "what time do you go on?"

Elsie went on first after intermission, and intermission

was then half over. For the first time in her life she was late. There was a fine flurry getting the Janises out of there, with Morgan calling the house doorman for their car and me calling the Palace to hold the curtain. As they left, Mrs. Janis turned in the doorway and levelled a finger at Morgan.

"*You* did this!" she accused him.

Irving Berlin was there that same evening, and I remember that he just retired to the piano and played soft music during the crisis.

I kept on working at *Vanity Fair* after my marriage, to the indulgent amusement of my husband who would come home from the Stock Exchange, find me batting out my monthly short-short on the typewriter, pat me on the head, and say, "Still writing away, Margie?" I don't know why I didn't kill him.

However, "writing away" was about the only thing I could do. I was pretty much of a flop as a stockbroker's wife otherwise. I could speak French, play the piano, swim, ice skate, drive a car, dance, and paint furniture without leaving any dried ripples, but—no matter how hard I tried—I could not learn the two requisites of being a stockbroker's wife. I could not play golf, and I could not play Bridge.

My mental block about Bridge brought out all of Morgan's true kindliness. He bought me a course of lessons with a Russian prince—I think his name was Alexei—who was operating as a Bridge teacher in New York. During the six-weeks course I reported glowingly to Morgan on my progress, and rather snootily informed our Bridge-playing friends that I would soon be able to (as Alexei put it) "take zem ovair ze coals."

One night Morgan and I and two of his Bridge couples,

the Haywards and the Roses, were dining at the Plaza when some other friends came in and stopped at our table. With them was a handsome young man who talked to me for quite a long time, flirtatiously, in French.

"Golly!" I said, when they had gone on to their own table, "*Who* was that divine man who was talking to me?"

"That," said Morgan, "was Prince Alexei, the Bridge teacher with whom you have been studying for the past six weeks."

So I never learned Bridge, and went on working for *Vanity Fair*. I liked my work, and besides, there was nothing for me to do at home, in our six-room apartment; it was all taken care of by a butler, a cook, a parlormaid, and a laundress. It took four people to take care of two people, in 1925.

It seems incredible now, but it is a fact that no young couple, in 1925, dared to set up housekeeping in a friendly community like Park Avenue without a staff of four; plus a nurse when the baby arrived, and a governess when the baby got too old for a nurse. No young mother ever took care of her own child, except on Thursday, the nurse's day off, and even then she began to feel slightly martyred toward the end of a long day. I remember one Thursday when I had fed our son and put him to bed, and was washing about a million diapers in the nursery bathroom, Morgan-my-husband appeared in the bathroom door wearing a new top hat, just arrived from Lock of London.

"How d'you like it?" he asked jauntily, preening himself in the long mirror of the bathroom door.

I told him without words. With one simple snarl I let fly a whole handful of wet diapers at the top hat. Knocked it off, too.

This show of temper was based neither on my dislike of

washing my son's diapers (I rather liked doing it), nor even on the horrid contrast between Morgan in his top hat and me with my hair in strings, but on the fact that washing diapers was a brand-new accomplishment for me and I wished to be congratulated on it. If Morgan had appeared in the bathroom door at that moment, top hat and all, and had said, "Still washing away, Margie?" who knows, we might still be married.

Actually, Morgan and I never had any fights during our four years of marriage; our life was so soft, so cushioned by servants and money that we never got close enough to each other to battle out any mutual problems. There *were* no problems, at least no financial ones. We entertained a good deal and, like other prosperous young men during Prohibition, Morgan prided himself on having a good cellar. A good cellar meant all kinds of drinks, not just wine, in those days. Our guests drank the best imported Scotch, and drank it with soda all through dinner, from soup to dessert. When our butler passed the tray of liqueurs later the guests were offered a choice of imported brandy, Cointreau, kummel, green chartreuse, yellow chartreuse, something called *lacrimae Christi*, and another thing I forget the name of that had a tree growing in the bottle. This was the custom; it was not considered vulgar, but it was expensive. Morgan and I spent fifty thousand dollars a year on just living, and we never owned anything. We never had a house in the country, or a boat, or even a piece of land, and the melancholy truth is that we never missed any of them. Young couples in the 'twenties were too busy paying rent and charge accounts and night-club checks to bother about investing in more permanent pleasures.

Considering the luxuriousness of life with Morgan, my astonishment was natural and unassumed when, soon after my return from Reno and our divorce, Constance Collier stopped me in the Algonquin lobby one day and murmured with utter sincerity, "Poor little gel, you've had a rather rugged time of it, haven't you?"

Recently I was talking to my daughter-in-law about the difference between present-day young couples and those in the 'twenties, as I sat in the kitchen of the house she and my son own in Lawrenceville and watched her whip up a soufflé with one hand and feed her two baby daughters strained carrots with the other. Through the open window drifted the sounds of hammering and an occasional curse from the lawn where my son, Case Morgan, was engaged in building a new terrace. He teaches English at Lawrenceville School, and builds things around the house on Saturdays and Sundays.

"I think young married people are just wonderful nowadays," I remarked dreamily. "So efficient and hardworking and unpretentious. In my day, a young wife couldn't do a darn thing except buy clothes, and we thought our husbands were big successes if they knew the right headwaiters and could always get a ringside table at a night club."

"So?" said Sheila. "Well, Maggie, since you're so crazy about hard work, how about putting down that cigarette and giving me a hand with Hilary's pants?"

"That's another thing," I went on, turning the youngest baby upside down, "I do so admire the respect, the tenderness, nay, even the reverence with which young wives address their mothers-in-law these days. Now, *I* was always terrified of Morgan's mother, I called her 'Mrs. Morgan' to the end of her days. It is refreshing to see this false homage replaced by the honest awe which you, for instance, display toward me."

Sheila, peering into the oven, made no reply beyond a soft sound with her lips, something like the whirring of tiny bird wings. But on my birthday, the following week, she sent me a birthday card depicting an ancient drab sitting over a bottle of gin with her hair falling in her eyes, and bearing the legend "Stay As Sweet As You Are" with the added inscription in ink: "Dear Mrs. Harriman, Sir; At last you get that pension! Yours respectfully, Mrs. Morgan."

Sitting in the Lawrenceville kitchen and intently admiring my granddaughter's feet, which are distinctly Case feet, I was reminded of Father, who was proud of his own long, narrow feet and took pleasure in the fact that mine, and my brother's, and my son's resembled them. Often, when we were swimming at Sag Harbor, he would line us up in a row on the dock with himself at the head and, with a certain dash, call the attention of the weekend guests to our arched, aristocratic and unblemished tootsies. This always called for a round of applause, only faintly derisive, followed by a respectful silence as Father pointed out that the second toe, longer than the big toe in all of us, was indisputably a mark of gentle birth. To my great delight, both my granddaughters, Lee and Hilary, have the same kind of foot.

Case came into the kitchen for a can of beer, and I asked him, "Remember when Frankie used to line us up on the dock at Sag and invite people to admire our feet?"

"Yes, and just think," said Case, "pretty soon I can do the same thing with my own daughters."

"You do, and I will personally pull the dock out from under all of you," promised Sheila, who had had enough of the Case Admiration Society. So, after only a passing reminder that Lee and Hilary are the ninth generation of

Cases in America, and probably the ninth to have a handsome foot, we kindly comforted Sheila for her own average second toe, and she cooked us a fine dinner.

Lightheartedness, thank heaven, is always a part of being young together, but Sheila's and Case's lightheartedness, it seems to me, is as dedicated as that of young salmon swimming upstream, whereas the gaiety of Case's parents in the 'twenties more resembled the antics of a water bug which covers a lot of ground and never gets anywhere much.

Cover ground we did. In 1926 a cable arrived from Father in London, asking Morgan and me to join him and Bud for a motor-tour of the English countryisde. We took the first boat and arrived in London almost, Father said later, before he had put down the pencil in the cable office. Edward Knoblock, the author of *Kismet*, *Milestones*, and other plays, had lent the Cases his house in Portman Square, adequately staffed with cook, butler, parlormaid and upstairs maid (yoo-hoo, Sheila!), but it was a small house, as houses go in England, and besides Father felt delicate about bringing his whole family into it. Therefore, he had engaged rooms for my husband and me at Brown's Hotel.

Brown's of blessed memory (it was destroyed by a bomb in World War II) was a few centuries older and considerably more famous than the Algonquin in New York, but English visitors to the Algonquin usually exclaimed on arrival, "It's the nearest thing to dahling Brown's!" Both hotels were small, very special, and crammed to the curb with celebrities, and since I was receptive to celebrities abroad to a degree I never felt at home, I was excited about staying there. My cup ran over when, as we entered, I glanced into the dark little dining room and saw a spectacled gentleman eating his dinner alone.

"Morgan," I whispered when we were upstairs in our rooms, "that man in the dining room was *Rudyard Kipling!*"

"Lousy hack writer," Morgan commented, "where the hell is the hot-water tap?"

There were no hot-water taps at Brown's, it turned out; hot water for baths and shaving was brought up to your room by a maid. "Just like Mrs. Hudson at 221b Baker Street!" I remarked delightedly, but Morgan had so many other remarks to make that mine were drowned out. The next day we moved, bag and baggage, to the Carlton and telephoned Father to give him our new address. This was probably the rudest thing anyone had ever done to Father —or to any other host—and I have always been sorry for it, but even after all these years I still take the wife's view: I loved Brown's and I loved my father, but I had to live with my husband.

Father, always the game loser, took us gaily off on the motor tour, during which Morgan complained that cathedrals were cold, English country was flat, winding roads had turns in them, and English pubs were unworthy of the name since they were not open to the public after hours. I used to look at him, wondering how this dream-man could be so obstreperous. How could I know, for he never told me and I was too artless to guess, that his crankiness derived only from the simple fact that he wished to be in Paris at the *Folies Bergères?*

Father's chauffeur was a Sicilian who had driven us through the château country in France a few years earlier. (Pa liked to have the same people work for him, whether in Europe or at home in New York.) Celestino was a good driver, hampered only by a total lack of any sense of direction and an accent, in all languages, so thick that it defied the finest ear.

"*La r-r-rrroute pour-rrr Tourrrrs!*" he used to demand in an angry shout of startled passers-by in some French town as he headed furiously in any direction exactly opposite to Tours. Now, in England, he was equally impatient with the good countryfolk.

"Cas-TEL! *Château!* he would yell suddenly at some innocent shepherd in a country lane, coming to a roaring halt one inch from the man's peaceful behind. He had it firmly fixed in his mind that his insane American passengers wished only to see châteaux, or cas-TELs, and he required at least one from every village we came to. It was an innocent shepherd, in fact, who gave Celestino the only backtalk I remember.

"Cas-TEL! *Château!*" Celestino screamed at this man, who paused to regard the irate Sicilian face thrust from the car window while his sheep placidly clogged the road around the car.

"We weesh cas-TEL! *Château!* We WEESH!" our driver hollered.

"Oh, ye do, do ye!" replied the peaceful relic. "Well, I wish you the same, dook, with knobs on and fringe 'anging all round." And he collected his sheep and passed quietly along the road.

Father enjoyed these little dialogues so much that he might have let Celestino battle his way through all England if the rest of us had not finally joined in the chauffeur's wish to see some cas-TELs. With a word or two, Father got us on the right road to Kenilworth, and in the shadow of that mighty castle I woke next morning with a fever and a slight rash, diagnosed by the local doctor as German measles. I had "German measles" off and on for the next few weeks, even back in London, and when we came home to New York I went to see the family doctor about it.

"German measles, my foot," he said, after examination. "You're just about six weeks pregnant, that's all."

Whenever my son recalls nowadays that he is partly English, at least by conception, he assumes the same baronial look I found so trying in his father when he tried on top hats. In vain I remind him that he might equally consider himself part German, since he was so long mistaken for a measle.

Happily for everyone, my son, Guion Case Morgan (he dropped "Guion" in his schooldays, sometime between Lawrenceville and Princeton) inherited his father's disposition, which generally was—and is—calm and even-tempered, and his grandfather Case's sense of humor. The combination has made him one of the most companionable people I know; small wonder, the psychiatrists might say, that with two such men in my family as my father and my son I have always had trouble finding a husband I thought equal to them. After Morgan and I were divorced, Guion (as I shall call him here for the present) lived with me, with periodic visits to his father, and spent all of his summers at Sag Harbor, growing up in the same house I had grown up in, and with the same people; Father and Bud, Sarah and Germaine. He always called Father "Frankie," and indeed it would have seemed absurd to address that slim, hoofing figure as "Grandpa." Soon Bud and I and the house guests began to follow suit, and "Frankie" Father remained from that time on. To Sarah, he was always "Boss," and Germaine, who watched over him like a mother, was about the only one to give him his full title, pronounced "Meestair Cayze." It was Germaine's idea that Frankie should wear heavier shorts in the cool weather toward autumn, and the only time I ever saw John Drew convulsed was one chilly day as he and Father were about to depart to a rather formal luncheon in Easthampton. A window overlooking the driveway was flung up as they got into the car, and Germaine leaned out and called shrilly, "Meestair Cayze! You 'ave NOT your PANTS!"

It was fine to see Guion come to know and love the same place, the same water, trees, house, people, and the small familiar rituals that had been so much a part of my own childhood. He could swim and dive and handle a boat almost as soon as he could walk, and not much later he was given charge of raising the flag on the sea wall first thing in the morning and lowering it at sunset—just as my brother Carroll had done. Two of our pet dinner-table rites also became great favorites with him. One was an old Bert Williams song Father used to warble whenever he rose to carve a roast of lamb:

> ". . . But the thing that tickles my palate the mos'
> IS lamb, lamb, LAMB!"

The other, also concerning lamb, was Father's French-Canadian story that began, "You take a nice, fat skonk, skin 'im up ti-i-ight . . ." and, proceeding with further elaborate instructions for preparing the skunk, ended with the whole family shouting, "I'd jus' as soon eat LAMB!" Today, at twenty-eight, Guion can still recite the nice-fat-skonk routine letter perfect.

He early developed a modest wit and an ear for music. Father had always been amused by a lifelong habit I had of cleaning my nails every night before I went to bed, and one night at Sag, Guion came into my room to say good night and found me doing this. He was up late that evening because we had gone into the village to see Walt Disney's movie of *Snow White and the Seven Dwarfs*.

"Why are you cleaning your nails before you go to bed? Nobody's going to wake you up in the middle of the night to look at 'em," he remarked with some scorn.

"You never know," I said sagely.

"Hmmm," he said, and then sitting down on the bed, sang thoughtfully to the tune of the "Snow White" waltz:

> "Some day my Prince will come,
> And search beneath my thumb . . ."

I caught the cue as he paused, and managed to come up with:

> "Is it clean? he'll want to know,
> Is my Snow White as white as snow? . . ."

Together, feeding each other inspirations, we finished it off:

> "Then he'll hand me a file,
> We'll dig a little while,
> If my nails are still dirty, then—oh, then—
> My Prince will not co-o-ome again."

Guion was about eleven then, but even at a much earlier age he had been full of surprises. In the summer of 1932, when he was only five, I married Jack Harriman, and owing to some technicality about Jack's previous divorce which forbade his remarrying in New York State, the ceremony was performed by a justice of the peace in Groton, Connecticut. Father gave us a handsome wedding breakfast at

Vasiliv

the Griswold Hotel in Groton, attended by both immediate families plus several dozen cousins and aunts and, naturally, Guion with his nurse. Halfway through the toasts and other festivities, Guion came pattering up to where I sat at the great table and whispered in my ear.

"Mummy," his baby lips confided, "the sheriff wants to see you."

I quickly excused myself and followed him into the corridor where the sheriff, or maybe it was the justice of the peace, was indeed jumping up and down. It seems he had just discovered that, although the marriage had been performed in Groton, where we were presently regaling ourselves, Jack had procured the license in the neighboring township of New London, and therefore we were not any more married than a monkey. What chiefly interested this official now before me was that he himself, as the New London authority, must re-perform the ceremony to make it legal, and that he had a golf date in exactly twenty minutes.

What to do? My dear ones and Jack's, some forty or fifty of them, were awash with gaiety, champagne and wedding cake in the next room, having a beautiful time. In fact the groom himself was having a beautiful time in the next room. Impossible for the bride to rush in with the fearful news that the thing was a mockery, and all was to do over again! Besides, there wasn't time. Families and friends alike had planned to take the four-o'clock back to New York, and it was then after three.

I will never know why the sheriff, or jay-pee, sent for me instead of summoning Jack—I have suffered much, during my life, from people's wrong-headed notion that I am a capable woman; but at any rate, I did the best I could on this occasion. I persuaded the dancing official to telephone

185

and postpone his golf game for a while, impressed upon Guion that his message from Ghent to Aix was a solemn secret until further notice, and he and I returned to the feast.

The next half hour was not made more comfortable for me by the succession of discreetly folded notes the sheriff, or jay-pee, kept sending me by the waiter. "We tee off at four o'clock promptly, it is now three twenty," the first one read. After that, he just wrote, "It is now 3:28," "It is now 3:36," and so on, until I began madly to expect the next note to read, "It is now midnight in Shanghai and noon in Moscow. At One Minute After Noon, I *shoot*." Not even all this nervous tension, however, could dampen my interest in the situation as I gazed around that roomful of happy, carefree people.

Here, I thought, was probably the only wedding breakfast in history at which no one but the bride is aware that she is living in sin.

The party broke up in the usual gay, last-minute scramble, and the dear ones took off on the four-o'clock as scheduled. All was peaceful as Jack and I settled into our Chrysler roadster, bound for honeymoon-land.

"Gosh, it's good to be alone with you! Here we go, darling!" he sang.

"Not just yet, dear," I was obliged to tell him. "We have to do something first."

"What do we have to do?" he demanded.

"We have to get married," I apologized.

Soon after our legal marriage in New London township Jack and I went, with Guion, to live in a small, darling stone house in New Canaan, Connecticut. We all spent a happy four years there.

And it was there, as Mrs. Harriman, that I learned for the first time what it is to be without any money at all.

People have always associated the name of Harriman with riches, as nobody knows better than I, who am still the victim of this popular delusion whenever I travel or buy something and give my name; the rate sometimes noticeably goes up. This is hard on me, a decently impoverished woman who would rather be known by my own name, Margaret Case, and am obliged to retain the "Harriman" to distinguish myself from the other Margaret Case, a society editor on *Vogue*.

Before Jack Harriman and I were married Jack cheerfully informed Father and me that he had no money except his salary from the firm of investment counselors where he worked, and these tidings failed to disturb us, since neither of us was known to be money-mad. Father and Guion immediately liked Jack, who was a big, booming kind of young man, six feet three and a yard wide, with an easy laugh and a way of coming into a room that seemed to move the walls aside and lift the ceiling. I guess it was charm. As for Jack's feeling for us, he was much more tolerant of the Cases than Morgan, who had once been known to remark, with some justice, "Trouble with those damn Cases, you have to keep 'em *amused* all the time. They don't think they're *living* unless they're laughing!"

Looking back, I feel a deep pity for the two men I tried to bring into the Case family through marriage. My mistake was, of course, in trying to bring them into the Case family instead of casting my lot with the families I had married into. But . . . do you wade when you can swim? Do you walk when you can fly? The Case family was more fun than anything, and I wanted the man I loved to belong to it. I never realized how tough it was for the man I loved. How impossible it was for a stranger, even though married to me, to be absorbed into a family so attuned to one another than an unspoken word could send us all into con-vulsions of laughter about nothing perceptible. We were never rude, but we were often guilty of the courteous pause which, to an outsider who is trying to catch up, is more shat-tering than a cut direct. We were, in fact, a closed corpora-tion, and our politeness only made it worse.

Jack Harriman came nearest to joining the Case family, simply by telling no jokes, painting the bathhouse at Sag Harbor (house guests who worked were always highly re-garded), and spreading charm all the way from the sea wall to the strawberry patch, five acres away. Jack was so charming that the strawberries were juicier than ever, that year.

The only Harriman I ever knew who had more charm than Jack was his mother, Grace Harriman. Her charm was true and effortless, like a child's. The first time I met her, after Jack and I were engaged, she instantly asked me to call her "Aunt Grace," and to call Jack's father "Uncle Ollie." After four years of calling my in-laws "Mr. and Mrs. Morgan," this friendliness dissolved me.

Anyone who ever knew Mrs. Oliver Harriman knows that her charm went deeper than mere friendliness. She was beautiful, gay, gallant, and—like the people I've tried to write about in this book—debonair. In the early years of her marriage to Uncle Ollie she had had great wealth, a town house in New York, country house in Westchester, the usual mansion in Newport, and all the horses, yachts, jewels, sa-bles and gowns that add up to riches. As the fortunes of Uncle Ollie's cousin, E. H. Harriman of the "railroad" branch of the family, rose, those of Uncle Ollie's branch, the "Wall Street Harrimans" dwindled, and when I first knew Aunt Grace and Uncle Ollie their only dwelling was a me-dium-sized New York apartment. After Uncle Ollie's death, and until her own death a few years ago, Aunt Grace lived alone in a small hotel on Gramercy Square. Such adjustments cannot be easy for a woman who has been a great beauty and a famous hostess and has loved every minute of it, yet I never saw anyone mourn departed money less than Aunt Grace did. She was always radiant, always ready to laugh, and forever busy with some large, improbable project or other. And to the end, she considered her husband and herself a cut above the "rich," or "railroad" Harrimans.

"Old E.H. was a rather tiresome man, you know," she told me once, arranging her silver-blue skirts on a pink couch and tucking in a curl of her silver-blue hair. "Ollie used to say to me, 'We must have him to dine, Grace,' and I would say 'Oh, *must* we?' because he generally took off his collar sometime during the evening, and he had a way of pinching the parlormaids, you know. Quite vulgar, really. But Ollie always said that much must be forgiven him because he was a financial genius, and so it proved to be. Of course his sons, both Averell and Roland, have turned out to be quite delightful young men, I believe, but alas!" Aunt Grace concluded without a trace of rancor, "we are far too poor these days to see much of them."

Aunt Grace—like Father, who became her firm friend— was a gregarious creature, and was happy in any surroundings as long as they included the people she liked. She could, and did, give a tea one afternoon for the then dowager Mrs. Vanderbilt (who, as I recall it, sat in a corner and received all comers with a rather clammy and birdlike claw), and the same evening, took Jack and me to dine with a double-cousin of hers, Grace Robinson, who lived with her husband in a tiny walk-up flat far north in the upper reaches of the West Side. Mrs. Robinson was cooking dinner when we arrived and, mingled with the appetizing odors of meat and vegetables, I noticed a faint, delicious aroma that surely came from no food. Aunt Grace noticed it too, and led us all into the kitchen.

"What are you cooking now, Grace?" she asked, lifting the lids off various kettles that stood bubbling on the back of the stove, behind the containers that held our dinner.

"Just some more of grandmother's old Kentucky recipes for face creams and lotions—*you* remember," said Mrs. Robinson. "I'll make you up a batch, if you like. In fact, I've been thinking I might put them on the market some-day, if I can ever find a big enough place to cook them."

Grace Robinson eventually did find a big enough place to "cook" them, and did put them on the market. As "Mary Chess" she operated her own perfume and cosmetics busi-ness for many profitable years before she sold it, a while ago, for over a million dollars.

If Aunt Grace Harriman was equally happy and at ease in a duchess's ballroom or a three-room walk-up flat, her son Jack carried his lack of social pretense to almost eccen-tric lengths. Having survived a polo-playing, younger-club-man's youth, he had resigned from Squadron A and from all clubs except the Racquet Club by the time I met him, and was indeed so addicted to simplicity that he once went through a whole weekend at Joe Hergesheimer's with a piece of string holding up his trousers because he couldn't find a belt or suspenders. His closest friends were a little group of deep thinkers who lived on Riverside Drive and, for some reason I never could fathom, always kept soiled white poodles as pets. This rarefied intellectual atmosphere was over my head, and I was glad when we moved to New Canaan where things were earthier. There I settled down happily as a suburban wife and mother, driving Jack to the train mornings and going to meet him at night, getting

Guion ready for the school bus, going down to the basement kitchen to discuss the marketing with The Black Panther, as Anna Pines, our cook and general toiler, was fondly known. Jack was reading "The Jungle Book" to Guion at the time, so he was Baloo, I was Riki-Tiki-Tavi, and Guion was, of course, Mowgli. That was about as intellectual as we got in New Canaan, except for the Thursday Afternoon Literary Club where the girls of the neighborhood met at various houses and read plays at one another, each one taking a different role. I was generally given the bitchy parts, since my N'Yawk accent was said to lend the proper nuance to the cattier lines.

Father and Bud, and Aunt Grace and Uncle Ollie often came out to Sunday dinner, and sometimes for the weekend. Guion grew and flourished like the pinks and tulips and roses in the garden, and my elderly Scotty, Topsy, after a preliminary bloodletting, fell in love with Jack's crazy young Irish setter and mooned over him like a dowager over a matinee idol. All was peace in New Canaan, and I blissfully did no writing whatever.

Father was happy about my translation from the night clubs to the nurseries (both botanical and progenical), and he had a pleasant habit of dashing off a note to me now and then, to say so.

> I am so glad you are taking an interest in flowers [he wrote, in one letter]. I don't think, at least I don't remember, ever seeing a flower until Bud called my attention to them, and yet I always loved to read about them, still think the words forsythia, delphinium, and larkspur are quite as lovely as the flowers themselves, maybe lovelier, for I do not yet know them by sight. Folks who do not know flowers and do not handle them are missing a lot of joy, I'm sure. Auntie Hinson,

every year with the first hint of Spring, would take a five-cent street car to the end of the line, then walk a mile or so and spend the whole day in the woods, returning at dark with a handful or so of poor, puny little things (our neighborhood wasn't much in the way of wildflowers), very tired and very happy. Always she asked me to go with her, and always I refused because I didn't know what it was all about. My mother who took no interest in flowers explained this lack by saying she had been too busy having babies (she had ten or a dozen) to bother about such things, and Auntie, who was no less a virgin than Holy Mary Mother of God—a bit more, if you ask me—for once had no comeback. A dirty trick that Mother never tired of pulling on her maiden sister.

Jack had the gift of treating Father as a contemporary, as I had always done, and as he loved to be treated; but the camaraderie appears to have reached a point at one time that worried me, for here is another letter from Father, in reply to one from me, contents forgotten:

> My darling,
> That is a perfect letter you wrote me, both in sentiment and expression, and I am so happy to get it. And please do not change your manner of treating me as "a contemporary and a friend". Between you and me, (although doubtless you have noticed it before now) I am extraordinarily vain about my autumnal crispness and independence. It would kill me to have anyone feel sorry for me or treat me with a little too much respect, either now or twenty years from now. You strike exactly the right note, and so does Jack.
> I am delighted and gratified with your letter.
> > Lovingly,
> > Father

Our idyllic existence in New Canaan might have gone on forever, but the year was 1933 and things were tough all over. Jack quit his job for a better one which failed to materialize, and we lived on the last of our bank account while he looked for another. Jobs were scarce for everyone in 1933, and nonexistent for a young man trained chiefly on the playing fields of Squadron A. Guion was all right—his father never faltered in his regular payments for his son's schooling, doctor's bills and clothing—but Jack and I were broke. We didn't want to appeal to our respective parents: Aunt Grace had already helped Jack more than once, and Father had slipped me a quiet check now and then, but in 1933 neither Harriman & Co. nor the Algonquin Hotel were doing much better than we were. "That was the year, I believe," Father remarked later, "when Bud and I lived alone in the hotel with the bus boys."

Jack sold his cuff links and eased his frustration by buying some oil paints and an easel and taking to the fields and byways to paint pictures, a thing he had always wanted to do. There was a rumpus about that, since I felt that the cuff-link money should have gone to the butcher, but Jack appeased me by charmingly presenting me, a few days later, with his first completed picture, a portrait of me. It was pleasing, except—as Jack said—"I can't seem to get that mean, grocer-bill squint out of your eye."

My squint probably became meaner as time went on and I sold my own gold cigarette case and the Steinway piano Father had given me when I married Morgan, and even hocked Morgan's square-cut-diamond engagement ring, to get enough money to keep the tradesmen quiet. I don't know why it had never occurred to me to seek a job in New York and commute with Jack, thus adding to the family income; I guess I was too happy with my little garden and my little stone house, and Mowgli, and the Black Panther, and too infatuated with my success at the Thursday Afternoon Literary Club, to want to leave any of it. Besides, I had inherited my father's strong conviction that riches do not matter, but a man must support his wife.

The day came, inevitably, when we had only one dollar in the bank, to keep the account open, eighty-seven cents in cash after I had searched all pockets and underneath all cushions, and no credit in the town. Not much food in the house, either, and about a gallon of gas in the car. I was near to despair, this day, and Jack was out painting in the fields, when the doorbell rang. I was afraid to answer it for a moment, expecting another creditor, but finally, like a cockeyed optimist, I opened it.

There, on the step, stood our old friend, Joseph Hergesheimer, wearing a suit of the finest English tweed, a Sulka shirt and tie, Charvet socks, Lobb shoes, and a Tyrolean hat with a feather in it. Nobody could have looked more expensive.

"Margaret!" Joe exclaimed, embracing me. "I've come to spend the weekend, and I'm starved!"

Any housewife will understand how truly glad I was to see dear Joe, and also how my mind immediately raced through the larder, and the amount of money on hand to replenish it. The answer to the last two problems was a double zero, but I was able to ignore it while I called Jack in from the fields (a euphemism I sometimes employed to make people think he was working), and while we all had a happy reunion. Presently Joe, the gourmet, said, "What are we having for dinner, Margaret? No, wait. . . . I'll tell you what I'd like. I'd like a broiled lobster with butter sauce and thinly sliced cucumber, fresh asparagus *hollandaise,* some toasted rye bread, and plenty of ale. Carling's Red Cap ale," he added strictly. "How does that suit you, Jack?"

"Wonderful!" said Jack, and gave me the husbandly look that means "Get It Done."

I excused myself and went to the telephone, which was fortunately in a small room with a door you could close. There I debated with myself for a moment. I couldn't possibly plead with the tradesmen any more; they wouldn't take it, nor could I. I couldn't invent any more "emergency" stories; they wouldn't believe them any more than I did. What to do? It never even crossed my mind to tell Joe that we were broke, and invite him to share our humble scrambled eggs. No, sir! In those medieval days of the nineteen-thirties, a noble who had richly fed you in his own castle and then turned up on the steps of your abode must be nobly fed in return, and not fobbed off with eggs and excuses. That was the rule.

I drew a long breath, called the store and asked for the manager, and adopted a deep, indignant tone.

"Look here!" I boomed. "This is Mrs. Harriman, and I want to give a rather large order, but it must be delivered more promptly than the last one, and there must be no confusion about the bill. Is that *clear.* Now, I would like three live lobsters, two fresh cucumbers, one pound of sweet butter, three bunches of fresh asparagus, three dozen bottles of Carling's Red Cap ale. . . . I beg your pardon. . . . Well, do you wish to deliver the order or do you *not?* . . . I thought so. Please repeat the order so far, and do not interrupt me again. . . . Right. Also, one four-rib roast of beef, five pounds of new potatoes, six bunches of endive, two heads of lettuce, one dozen tomatoes. . . ."

It worked. The goods arrived, on credit, and we ate well that weekend and for several days afterward. My son, who must have overheard me on the phone that day, maintains that I still use the Mother-has-spoke, parade-ground voice on the telephone when I feel that things are going against me, and he may be right. To anyone to whom I have ever used that voice, and who has objected to it, I can only say that it is the voice of desperation; be gentle with it.

After my success with the tradesmen, we were naturally worse off financially than ever, and one day I was plunged into even deeper gloom when I chanced to look up a friend in my address book and found two people on the same page who had died during the past year.

"These people are *dead!*" I cried to Jack, who had come in from the fields to lunch. The news left him calm, since he hadn't known them anyway, but it haunted me until I finally sat down and wrote a very short, very sad story called "New York Is Just A Village." It was all about how you never know your neighbors in New York until suddenly, when you want them, they're dead, and it was one of those pieces written in great melancholy that turn out to be perfectly hilarious. I sent it to the *New Yorker*, who bought it and paid me fifty dollars for it. The fifty took care of Joe's weekend with something left over, and I began to rest easier. Pretty soon a letter came from the *New Yorker*, saying "Why don't you write some more pieces for us? Why not try your hand at a Profile?" The letter was signed "Affectionately, Katharine."

Katharine Angell was a woman I had met in 1929 when we were both staying at a guest-ranch outside Reno. She was a small, slender, rather serious gal who spent most of her time at the ranch alternately reading miles of galley proof sent to her from *The New Yorker*, where she was an editor, and trying to make up her mind whether to marry a certain person back in New York who also worked on the magazine. We had lost touch with each other since our return from Reno (New York *is* just a village), and now she had married the certain person, and her name was Katharine White. I imagine she never really had any grave doubts about her decision, and their enduring marriage and her husband's present eminence as a writer prove that she made no mistake in choosing E. B. White.

After a telephone consultation with Katharine I wrote a Profile of Uncle Don, a radio character who had been driving me mad for some time, owing to my son's passion for listening to him at six o'clock every evening when I wished to listen to something else. This undertaking involved many trips to New York to interview folksy old Uncle Don in his plain old penthouse, and *The New Yorker* bought the Profile and paid two hundred and fifty dollars for it. After another Profile (Mary Pickford) I was given a regular job writing the "Out of Town" department, which I accomplished mainly by calling up everybody I knew who had ever been to Bermuda, the Laurentians, or other resorts, and demanding to be told the thrilling details. I also wrote the "Tables for Two" column for a while, when Lois Long was on vacation, and continued to turn out Profiles, Reporter pieces, and casuals at a fairly prolific rate. In the next few years *The New Yorker* voluntarily increased my pay from the original two hundred and fifty dollars a piece to about seven times that amount, and I mention this fact only because each raise always touched me deeply. Happy though I had been working for *Vanity Fair*, the Condé Nast Publications believed firmly in impressing upon its contributors the joys of working for "prestige" rather than money, and the incredible luck of any young writer accepted by *Vanity Fair* or *Vogue* in having such a showcase for his talents. Writers got none of this smooth-talk from *The New Yorker*. If you kept on working for *The New Yorker*, and your work improved, you got paid accordingly.

In spite of this openhandedness, no Profile writer of my acquaintance ever got rich on Profiles; due partly to the generally indigent character of Profile writers, but also attributable to the system known as the Drawing Account. On a drawing account with *The New Yorker*, you received a weekly check from the magazine to cover living expenses, and you wrote against it. If you turned in a piece for which you were to be paid a thousand dollars, say, and you had collected only five hundred from the drawing account while writing it, you got a check for the other five hundred. If, on the other hand, you had already received a thousand dollars from the drawing account, you got nothing, except the weekly check toward future pieces. If you were behind with your work, and were into the drawing account for money advanced which you had not yet earned, the drawing account did not stop. The weekly check continued until you owed *The New Yorker* money which you were in honor bound to work out. This accounted for a good many neuroses in Profile writers, and also for a good deal of superior writing. When the rent is overdue, a writer writes harder and faster, and probably better, than when the going is easy.

Harold Ross, editor and psychologist, knew this. Once, when I myself was deep in the hole about my drawing account, I asked him why he didn't put a limit on the amount a writer could draw without producing enough pieces to pay for the overdraft.

"Don't have to," said Ross. "Writers are conscientious people in spite of themselves; that's one of their troubles. You tell a writer his drawing account is good up to a thousand dollars, he'll get in hock for a thousand dollars, and then leave you and worry about it for the rest of his life. You've lost the thousand dollars, but you've also lost the writer. But tell him his drawing account is unlimited, and before he's in hock to the magazine for a thousand dollars, he flies into a private panic and goes to work. We lose fewer writers and get more pieces that way," Ross concluded peacefully.

As for me, after that little chat, I went home and went to work.

You might have thought that, with money again coming in regularly, our domestic scene would have regained its former bloom, but it didn't work out that way. In 1936, Guion and I and the Black Panther, along with our Scotty, reluctantly parted from Jack Harriman and took up housekeeping in a modest apartment in New York. On account of the Harriman name (there it is again) the newspapers carried stories of the divorce, most of them headlined "Mrs. Harriman Asks No Alimony." It was then that I came to revere Maury Paul, the original "Cholly Knickerbocker" of the Journal-American. Mr. Paul's story simply inquired "WHAT alimony?" and added, "Margaret Case Harriman earns more in a month than Jack Harriman has ever earned in a year." This was brisk, but true, and I admired him for being one gossip columnist who knew what he was talking about.

I never met Mr. Paul until the following year, when *The New Yorker* assigned me to do a Profile about him. I called him up and we made a date for lunch in the Ritz Japanese Garden, and there I unwittingly won his favor just as he had won mine. We ordered lunch, and I added to the waiter, "I'd like some toast, but not Melba toast. I want some good thick slices of hot toast, *this* thick," and I held my fingers about an inch apart to demonstrate.

Maury Paul leaned back in his chair and regarded me. "You like your toast thick?" he asked.

"I sure do, and I always have to ask for it that way," I said.

Mr. Paul nodded, and bent forward to pat my hand.

"You'll *do!*" he said seriously. "One thing I like is *daring!*"

* Chapter 8 *

HAROLD ROSS, founder and editor of *The New Yorker*, was a lean and rangy man whose furrowed brow gave him a perpetual look of harassment. He walked with a preoccupied gait, shoulders hunched forward as if leaning into an opposing wind, and he was furthermore a man who was always plainly astonished when anything pleasant happened to him. One day he took me to lunch at Voisin to discuss future Profiles, and as he paid the check and we prepared to leave, he reared back and stared at me.

"Say!" he exclaimed in utter surprise. "You know, I *enjoyed* this lunch?"

He claimed that writers were his sorest trial, and if this was true, he had a quality that was Job-like; for he never, with one exception, outwardly lost patience with them. The exception was Alexander Woollcott, whose frequent tantrums and stormy resignations caused gray hairs among all of *The New Yorker* staff. In the interest of sanity for all concerned Ross finally and firmly accepted one of Woollcott's resignations.

Some theorists have maintained that the success of *The*

New Yorker was due to the fact that Ross was a small-town boy from Aspen, Colorado, and that his viewpoint toward the big city remained naïve, and therefore fresh. Ross always indignantly contradicted this surmise, pointing out that he had left Aspen at an early age and had ever since been (in his own words) "the petted darling of world capitals." It is a fact that, from the age of nineteen, he had held newspaper jobs in Salt Lake City, Sacramento, New Orleans and San Francisco, and in 1918, when he was twenty-six and a private in the 18th Engineers of the A.E.F., found himself in Paris and on the staff of the *Stars and Stripes*, the Army newspaper. It was probably here that the seeds of *The New Yorker* took root, when Ross found himself a colleague of such newspaperman as Franklin P. Adams, John T. Winterich, Hudson Hawley, A. A. Wallgren, C. Leroy Baldridge, and—as a final and flossy touch—Sergeant Alexander Woollcott who was, in civilian life, drama critic of *The New York Times*.

As an extremely roving reporter Ross had long had his eye on New York, and after the war it was, oddly enough, a fashion magazine named *Delineator* which brought him there. The Butterick Publishing Company, which owned *Delineator*, had heard of the notable success of *Stars and Stripes* (of which Ross had become managing editor), and wished to engage its entire staff to set up a civilian magazine, addressed mainly to ex-soldiers, to be called *The Home Sector. The Home Sector* lasted for only four issues before merging with the *American Legion Weekly*, with Ross as editor of the combined magazines. Five years later, in 1924, he became editor of *Judge*, the old comic weekly —a position which unnerved him somewhat, since he claimed that nobody on *Judge* ever had a single original idea all the time he was there, and furthermore that *Judge* never paid its contributors until threatened with the law. Ross had married Jane Grant, a newspaperwoman whom he had met in Paris during the war, and to calm himself, he used to take Jane for long walks around New York on Sundays and talk about his own pet idea of a humorous weekly about New York, addressed particularly to New Yorkers. During his twenty-six years as head of *The New Yorker*, until his death in 1951, Ross never deviated from his original tenet that the magazine should be strictly local in appeal. Once I cabled him from Paris, expressing my annoyance at not being able to find a copy on Parisian newsstands. "So what?" he cabled back. "We aren't writing it for Parisians."

The story of *The New Yorker* has been told before (by me, among others), but another brief account may be excusable here, in a book mainly about the Algonquin, since the magazine came into being chiefly at the daily luncheon sessions of the Algonquin Round Table attended by Ross, Woollcott, Adams, Broun, Benchley, Dorothy Parker, Marc Connelly, Frank Sullivan, and other literary friends of the project. Further intellectual encouragment was offered by Alice Duer Miller, Ralph Barton, Katharine Angell and Rea Irvin; and financial help was promised by Raoul Fleischmann of the baking family, with a good prospect of more money from Fleischmann's wealthy cousin, Julius Fleischmann. Ross thought that fifty thousand dollars would do as a starter, and he and Jane had already raised half that amount.

The first issue came out in February, 1925. Three weeks later, Julius Fleischmann died suddenly while playing polo and, unfortunately, before he had contributed anything to the magazine's support. Raoul Fleischmann, depressed by his cousin's death, showed signs of weakening about the whole thing, and, that spring, things got so bad that Ross seriously considered suspending publication while he looked for another backer. *The New Yorker* was saved by two unexpected allies: the calendar, and the power of the press. Its publication date had just been changed by advancing it three days, thus making a ten-day interval between issues; during the extra three days, Raoul Fleischmann decided to continue his support—and *The New Yorker* was again fairly secure financially. Also, Alice Duer Miller had sent a young cousin of hers to see Ross with a piece she had written, called "The Stag Line." Ross published it, with the name of the author, Ellin Mackay, at the end as usual, and the piece and its author (and incidentally, *The New Yorker*) made headlines in all of the newspapers the following day. "Daughter of Clarence Mackay Raps Social Conventions" the papers blared, and "Socialite Deb Goes to Town in *New Yorker* Magazine." When, the following year, Ellin Mackay married Irving Berlin the papers, a-revel in the unusual romance, still found time to refer to the bride's former piece in *The New Yorker*, and to quote excerpts from it. It did *The New Yorker* no harm.

No grand publicity, nor any whim of the calendar, could have saved a magazine that was not good to begin with; but *The New Yorker* was a good magazine, and those two episodes were its turning point.

To be sure, *The New Yorker*, at first, was not nearly as good as it later became. Its early issues were skimpy and faintly collegiate in tone. Ross, with the picture of perfection in his mind's eye, worried so constantly about the magazine that he got into the habit of worrying about everything, and the sight of him pacing his shabby office with wrinkled brow became a familiar one to his staff.

Once, during this pacing, a subeditor ventured to ask him what was the matter *now*, and Ross came to a desperate halt.

"Goddamit," he explained, "we got to have a *water cooler* in here!"

Ross's worries, which eventually produced the ulcer that forced him to a milk diet, would fill a book, and have done so. It is enough to say here that *The New Yorker*, starting with a capital of fifty thousand dollars, was appraised, in the year of his death, at a stock value of ten million.

The New Yorker, when I began writing for it in 1934, had two methods of assigning Profiles, both very liberal toward the Profile writer. A writer could suggest a subject and, if the editors approved it, go ahead and submit his first draft of the piece. This was where liberality ended and hard labor began. I have written elsewhere of the toil entailed in writing Profiles, of the editors' queries, the checkers' queries, and the endless rewriting, so I will merely say here that an apprentice Profile-writer usually got by on his fifth or sixth version, a veteran often on only his second or third. The other, equally liberal method of assignment involved a large black ledger listing a hundred or so names of people in public life whom the editors considered to be likely Profile material. That the color of this ledger was black was incidental, and signified no preconceived editorial opinion of the subjects. A writer who had no suggestions of his own at the moment could ask for the Black Book and, running through its columns, cry "Ooh! I'll take *that* one!" His next step, after the assignment was approved, was to telephone or write to the subject and make a date to meet.

There was never any trouble about that. A Profile,

whether a nosegay or a needling, was the accolade, and no public figure was too exalted or too modest to want one. Our subjects were generous with their time and attention, allowing us to follow them around as closely and as long as was necessary—sometimes for days, sometimes for weeks —and freely suggesting other sources of information among their friends and associates. To get a complete picture a Profile writer had, of course, to interview half a dozen people who knew and loved the subject, and another half dozen who knew and hated him, and the latter group we usually had to ferret out for ourselves. That the whole procedure was almost invariably pleasant and even entertaining for all concerned I attribute largely to the fact that no Profile writer was ever known to pull out a notebook and pencil—a gesture which is sure to paralyze even the most willing interviewee. An occasional unobtrusive note on the inside of a matchbook-cover was all right, but you kept your paper and pencil well hidden and merely listened and encouraged until you had all that your tiny mind could hold for one day. Then (at least, this was my own system) you beat it to a taxi, hopped in, whipped out the pencil and pad—or more likely, several sheets of folded yellow copy paper—and wrote it all down on the way home, before you forgot it. It was wise to transcribe these notes on a typewriter while you could still read them, since they usually looked something like, "chd C pk W, anec G-fat & Me. trap.," meaning, when unravelled, that the subject's childhood had been passed on Central Park West and that there was an anecdote about his grandfather and a Maine trapper.

Amid all this camaraderie there was bound to be an occasional sour note. One lady tycoon to whom I was assigned changed her story so often that I at last appeared

dizzily before Harold Ross. "That dame has told me so many lies I don't know what she's talking about!" I wailed. Ross kindly relieved me of the assignment. Another time Mike Todd, the producer, invited me to dine with his wife and himself at their apartment for our first meeting. When I arrived he was alone, wearing striped pajamas and a dressing gown and chewing a fat cigar. I never finished that Profile either. But my darkest failure was with Miss Virginia Gildersleeve, then Dean of Barnard College. I arrived at her office for our first interview wearing my usual working clothes which, on this day, included a little black thing of a hat with a nose-veil, and a small black beauty patch I was in the habit of pasting on the left cheekbone. Dean Gildersleeve looked at me, frowned, and asked if I were a college graduate.

"No," I admitted. "I went to school in France instead. But," I added hopefully, "I *did* pass my entrance exams for Vassar!"

This seemed the wrong thing to say. Dean Gildersleeve slowly surveyed me from toe to top, and sighed.

"They might at least have sent a college graduate to interview me," she said.

"I'm sorry," I murmured.

"In fact, I had hoped *The New Yorker* would send a *man* to interview me," the Dean went on. "Why *didn't* they send a man?"

I had already apologized for going to school in France, now I was asked to apologize for being a woman, and this, coming from our beloved educator and champion of women's rights, was too much for me.

"Probably for the same reason they haven't got a man as Dean of Barnard College," I snapped.

We got along better after that, and I really tried to write

that Profile. I put an extra amount of work and research into it, but my heart wasn't in it, and my first draft came back from *The New Yorker* with twelve pages of editors' queries (instead of the usual three or four pages), ending with the despairing pencilled cry from Ross, "Gildersleeve *must* be more interesting than this!" I was gently relieved of that assignment too, and nobody to my knowledge ever dared take it on again. Come to think of it—and I just checked with *The New Yorker*—no Profiles were ever published of the lady tycoon, Mike Todd or Dean Gildersleeve, so perhaps they frightened other writers as well.

Apart from those three catastrophes, my recollections of Profile writing are sunlit. All the associations were lively, and little things happened from time to time which delighted me, but did not fit into the rigid form of the Profile. For instance;

Leland Hayward asked me to lunch at Twenty-One for an interview and, calling for a table telephone to be plugged in, made transatlantic and coast-to-coast calls to various pals throughout the meal. When I at last complained of this neglect he said, "Gee, you're patient! When I did the same thing to Edna Ferber one time, she dumped her vegetable plate in my lap and walked out."

Max Gordon, on the other hand, kicked like a steer when I asked him to lunch at the Algonquin and signed the check myself. "You can't do this!" he cried. "At least let me buy you a cigar?" Max was also the only Profile subject I ever knew who said to me enthusiastically, "I'll give you the address of a fella to go and see who'll be a great source of material for you. He hates me!"

Sometimes I took my son Guion along with me on interviews, where he behaved with decorum and insight. From Rouben Mamoulian, the stage director, he obtained several valuable pointers on how to put on the Spring Show at Lawrenceville, where he was newly enrolled; and when he lunched at the Algonk with Emily Post and me, Mrs. Post, who had brought up two sons and knew how to get on with boys, made such fast friends with him that I could hardly get a word in edgewise. A week or so later she asked us both to tea at her apartment in the East Seventies, and gave us a fine country tea with toasted, buttered English muffins and strawberry jam—delicious, but difficult to eat daintily from a small plate in one's lap. Mrs. Post is one of the easiest companions in the world, but nevertheless there are few people who do not suffer, in her presence, a slight self-consciousness about their own ease of manner. Not so my young son. When he dropped his muffin butter-side-down (fortunately on his plate, not on the carpet), he merely said, "Oops," picked it up, and started over again. Mrs. Post afterward told me that this one small incident illustrated the whole of her teachings on etiquette. "For more than twenty years I have been urging people just to be natural," she said, adding with a sigh, "I guess nobody can do it, except children."

"Or great actresses like Helen Hayes," I suggested.

"Or great actresses like Helen Hayes," Mrs. Post agreed.

The process of my doing a Profile of Helen Hayes brought out a little-known quality in Harold Ross, a man seemingly pictured by the reading public as an assassin with a cleaver, waiting to decapitate the innocents. This notion was as far from the truth as the other popular delusion, that a Profile was necessarily an assassination. Ross was a fair-minded editor who disliked the blurbs that had passed for magazine biographies until he came along, and who believed that an accurate and interesting account of a person must speak of his faults as well as his virtues; but he was no less insistent on a writer putting in the virtues then he was on including the faults. If a Profile writer, carried away by phrase-making, wrote a line or a paragraph which seemed to him hilarious or witty but which was not strictly fair, Ross's editorial comment on this passage would read: "Delete? Seems gratuitous." When a Profile concerned someone whom he knew and truly admired, he became so far removed from the man with the cleaver, so violently a champion in plumes and armor, that he could be, and sometimes was, a nuisance to his writers. This happened about Helen Hayes, whom I admired no less than Ross did.

In my first draft I had written of Miss Hayes, honestly enough: "She is not beautiful in the classic sense, and actors who have worked with her believe that this has something to do with her being a good actress. 'Take Ina Claire,' they say. 'She's wonderful, all hair and figure and personality, but she's always Ina Claire; Lynn Fontanne the same way. Helen has no glamour—her face is just a face that reflects things—but how she can *give* a character!' In this statement, the word 'give' is accompanied by a clenching and curving of the hand and a sharp jerk upward."

A day or so after I turned in this first draft I went to dinner at the Algonk with Father and Bud, and was only halfway into my chair when I was hailed by Ross, who was dining across the room.

"How do you mean, Helen Hayes is not beautiful?" he roared.

I excused myself to the family and went over to Ross's table. After all, he was my boss, and besides Father didn't like plumed knights riding helter-skelter across his restaurant, especially during the dinner hour.

"How do you mean, how do I mean Helen Hayes is not beautiful?" I asked.

Ross ordered a chair brought for me, introduced me to his table companions (I have forgotten who they were), and when everything was nice and cosy, leaned forward and smote me broadsides.

"I read your piece today. You say that Helen Hayes is not beautiful. This is bad reporting."

To fully appreciate the impact of that statement the reader must understand that the only real crime, with Ross and *The New Yorker*, was bad reporting. To a *New Yorker* writer, being accused of bad reporting was equivalent to a soldier's being stripped of his insignia and drummed out of the regiment.

I reeled, but recovered sufficiently to protest, "I didn't say that Helen Hayes was not beautiful. I said she isn't beautiful in the classic sense."

Ross's friends supported me, and he waited until we had finished agreeing with one another. Then he said, "Listen. Helen Hayes is a beautiful woman, and any reporter who says she isn't is a goddam bad reporter." With which he took a swig of milk (his only potion at the time) and glared at me.

Father, at this point, sent me a note with the familiar, fatherly command, "Come to dinner!"

In the next week it took me three separate conferences with three separate *New Yorker* editors—McKelway, Gibbs, and one named Sanderson Vanderbilt—before Ross and I could be brought to a meeting of minds about Miss Hayes's looks. Ross still maintained that she was beautiful in every sense, and I still held my ground that she was not classically beautiful. It was McKelway who finally found a solution by suggesting that I cut four words and insert one.

In the second draft of the Profile the passage, now satisfactory to both Ross and me, read; "She is not strikingly beautiful, and actors who have worked with her believe . . ." et cetera. The rest of the paragraph remained intact.

The thing that interests me about this episode, looking back on it, is that Ross never quarreled with the only outrageous statement I made concerning Helen Hayes. To be sure, it wasn't my own, but I quoted fellow actors as saying "She has no glamour." Ross and I were so busy wrangling about Miss Hayes's type of beauty that neither of us ever noticed this blazing misstatement of fact.

The third, and next-to-final draft of the Hayes Profile was returned to me with several further, and justified, complaints from Ross, but also with a note which, as always, took the sting out of the everlasting rewriting. "This piece is too good not to be perfect," he wrote simply.

Like many literary men who are taken up socially by people in society and politics, Ross became in time a little class conscious; by that I mean that he was anxious to establish himself as a man of no affectations whatever. One day, he came into an office where I was going over proofs of a Profile with Sanderson Vanderbilt.

"Missus Harriman and Mister Vanderbilt," muttered Ross, fretting in the doorway. "What am I running here, a magazine or a goddam Social Register?"

Of the thirty or forty Profiles I wrote for *The New Yorker* only four—Mary Pickford, Leland Hayward, Clare Boothe and Fanny Holtzmann—were about anyone I had ever met before, and almost none of the others led to any lasting friendship between the subject and me. An exception was Richard Rodgers, or so I like to think. Along with the rest of the nation I had loved his music since the first *Garrick Gaieties*, and I was happy to discover, when I came to write about him and his then partner, Larry Hart, that his songs were no more engaging than he was. Dick's approval of me began, perhaps, on the night *I Married an Angel* opened, when a group of us, after the show, were discussing which numbers we liked best (the title song, or *Spring Is Here*, et cetera), and I happened to remark that I liked "the music where the angels came down." Dick beamed at me. "Maggie, you always say the right thing," he murmured. Since the angel music was merely incidental, nobody else had paid much attention to it, but I have ever been addicted to background themes; preferring, for example, the counterpoint in Gershwin's *Mine* to the tune itself.

Another reason I am fond of Mr. Rodgers is that he was twice instrumental in saving my life, or at least in prolonging it. The first time occurred in 1932 when I was gravely ill and delirious in St. Luke's Hospital and (they told me later) kept talking wildly about dancing on the ceiling. The doctors and nurses thought I was raving, but Father, who knew better, brought in a portable phonograph and a record of *Dancing on the Ceiling*, the Rodgers and Hart tune from a London show called *Evergreen*. It may not have been the song alone that cured me, but I certainly began to get better right away.

Mr. Rodgers' second gesture in my direction was even more personal, and involved some physical bravery. At a party he and his wife, Dorothy, gave to celebrate their sixteenth wedding anniversary I wore a new black evening hat with a little nose-veil. As I lit a cigarette, the flame of the match touched the veil and in an instant the whole hat and part of my hair were on fire. With one bound Dick and Mady Christians, who were sitting near me, sprang forward, ripped off the burning hat, and put out the fire in my hair with their bare hands. A composer's hands, and an actress's hands, are important to them; but neither Dick nor Mady hesitated for a second.

Dorothy Rodgers and Eleanor Holm led me away to the powder room to brush off the cinders, and Miss Holm, who was then married to Billy Rose, borrowed scissors from the maid and shaped my scorched hair into a new and quite becoming bang. Her husband's attitude toward the whole episode was less kindly but even more striking. He had been sitting on the end of his spine on a sofa nearby when I caught fire, and he continued to sit there throughout, casting only an indifferent eye upon the conflagration.

"That Billy Rose!" I said indignantly to Dick a bit later on. "I could have shot flames ten feet high and burned to a crisp at his very feet before *he'd* move a muscle!"

"He might not have stirred, even then," said Dick. "Probably he would have figured it was just a rival spectacle staged by Mike Todd."

Lillian Hellman, another Profile subject, also became a stimulating and forthright friend for a while, before she grew to be so politically minded. But Lillian and I disagreed on more than politics. One night after dinner at her apartment along with (as I recall it) Dorothy Parker, Louis Kronenberger and Herman Shumlin, the talk turned to another friend of mine, Katherine Brush, who had written "Young Man of Manhattan" and "Red Headed Woman," among many popular novels. I remarked that I thought she was a good writer, and the intellectuals turned to me incredulously. "What's good about her?" somebody demanded.

"Well, I think she's good at drawing a character incisively in a very few words," I said. "For instance, just by suggesting that a woman doesn't bathe daily, she can put across the idea to the reader that this dame is pretty much of a slob in every way."

This was greeted by hoots and catcalls from the company assembled, and Lillian and Mrs. Parker were so moved that they crossed the room and stood before me.

"Do you mean to sit there, Maggie Harriman," cried Lillian, "and say that you think that if a woman doesn't take a bath every day there's something the matter with her?"

"I certainly think that personal sloppiness can indicate a sloppy mind and a sloppy character," I insisted.

"Do *you* take a bath every day?" cooed Mrs. Parker dangerously.

"Of course I do. Doesn't everybody?"

"Prize fighters," Mrs. Parker murmured with disdain, and I was dismissed as a mere fusspot. Or possibly, as someone suggested, a fusspot with a guilt complex which drove me to incessant washings.

It was later that same evening that someone asked Louis Kronenberger what title he had chosen for the new book he was writing.

" 'Kings, Queens, and Desperate Men' " said Louis.

"Go Out in the Mid-day Sun," I added irresistibly, as who wouldn't? For this I was branded flippant. A flippant fusspot with a guilt complex. I am positive that this slight exchange in no way influenced Louis to change his title, as he later did, to "Kings and Desperate Men."

In 1934, *The New Yorker* had achieved such prestige that any young writer appearing in its pages was instantly approached by other magazines, and I was no exception.

Since I was a free-lance writer with no contract anywhere, I happily wrote for *Good Housekeeping,* the *Saturday Evening Post* and other national magazines at twice the price I got from *The New Yorker,* and at one half the pains. Ross did not care for these deviations on the part of his writers, and often made pointed remarks about the nasty glitter of gold, and how all writers were money-crazy; but he did not fret too much about it. He knew the truth: once a *New Yorker* writer, always a *New Yorker* writer. And it is a fact that, no matter how cushioned by more liberal and easygoing editors, I—for one—always preferred to work for Ross.

He was a kind man, as well as a tough one. In 1936, I was offered a free trip to Europe by the French Tourist Bureau, along with some other "*journalistes.*" I lacked only pocket money—this was before I began to write for the large-paying magazines—and I couldn't ask my father for money; partly because he and the Algonquin were going through the Depression, and mostly—perhaps—because I was too proud, having supported myself for two years. I went to Ross and asked him to advance me four hundred dollars for pocket money on the trip.

"Certainly," said Ross, and wrote out a check for four hundred dollars which I was able to cash immediately.

"You might be able to write a piece for us in France," he said thoughtfully. "I hear that Pearl White, the old serial queen, is still living in the south of France somewhere. If you run across her, you might write a piece about her for us. Sort of Where Are They Now kind of thing."

"No!" I said violently. "I am supposed to go to France to write about *France*—not about some dead old silent-movie queen!"

I paid off the four hundred dollars as soon as I got home, from the seven hundred and fifty I was paid for my next Profile. I got one hundred and fifty for a piece I wrote about France, for *Vogue*. It added up to five hundred dollars in cash, all I had in the world. I went to bed, one night, a failure, and didn't sleep very well.

Next morning I was wakened by Ross on the telephone. "How about some more pieces?" he said. "We've arranged to pay you a little more."

The "little more" was eight hundred dollars for a one-part Profile, and one thousand for a two-part Profile. It soon became one thousand for one part, and eighteen hundred for two parts. Ross never paid double for a two-part Profile, or triple for one in three parts. I never asked why. It was less than I got, later, from the national magazines, but I was happy with it. Like most writers, I got a peculiar joy out of writing for *The New Yorker*.

When Ross died, unexpectedly in 1951, a simple service was held at Campbell's Funeral Parlors on Madison Avenue. Nobody thought there would be much of a crowd, so the funeral took place in a small chapel. When I arrived, ten minutes before the service began, the chapel was filled, the standing room was filled, and a hundred more people lined the steps and the sidewalk, waiting to get in. A harried attendant passed me, with furrowed brow.

"Goddamit," he whispered to a subordinate, "we got to get some *chairs* in here!"

I think Ross would have liked that.

* Chapter 9 *

MANY young people, impelled by their own mad mathematics, are inclined to associate everybody over forty exclusively with the nineteen-twenties. They look at a woman of forty-five and say, "My! She must have been real cool in the 'twenties!" forgetting that, in 1920, for example, she was exactly eleven years old. I don't mind admitting to any finger-counters present that I was no eleven years old in 1920, but I was still in my own twenties in the nineteen-thirties, and I somehow think of them as the days of my youth. Musing upon this and like matters the other day when I had just absently thrown a pair of nylon stockings out of the bathroom window and dropped a lighted cigarette butt into the laundry hamper, I was inspired to the following (hitherto unpublished) lines:

> O, Life that leaves its lines on faces,
> And strangely alters other places,
> Could you not humanly instead
> Wither and shrink my *other* head?

The nineteen-thirties were a time of national depression
—and for me, of occasional penury and even illness—yet I,
along with many other people my age, remember them as
rosy. We were all young, but it was not only that; there
were good things all around us. The theatre, for one. Isn't
it truly remarkable how, in times of darkest financial stress,
the theatre always shoots forth its brightest blossoms, like
flameweed growing out of some old neglected stump?
Producers, playwrights and actors seem to work so well in
adversity that I cannot see how the great artists of the
Renaissance ever got anything done, with all those patrons
making life so cushy for them.

The 'thirties were the great days, in the theatre, of
*Grand Hotel, The Barretts of Wimpole Street, Reunion in
Vienna, Private Lives, Dinner at Eight, The Animal King-
dom, The Children's Hour, The Petrified Forest, Vic-
toria Regina, Idiot's Delight, Outward Bound, The Man
Who Came to Dinner*, and *Life with Father*—to name
only a few plays of the decade; of such grand musical
shows as *Three's A Crowd, Roberta* (featuring a young
leading man named Bob Hope), *As Thousands Cheer,
Anything Goes* and *The Boys from Syracuse*. The movies
were almost as good: *Rasputin and the Empress*, with all
three Barrymores, *Of Human Bondage*, which made Bette
Davis a star, *It Happened One Night, Berkeley Square*
. . . and all the wonderful "team" pictures; Ginger-Rogers-
and-Fred-Astaire, William-Powell-and-Myrna-Loy, Mau-
rice-Chevalier-and-Jeanette-MacDonald (although I personally always preferred Chevalier by himself on a stage).

The popular songs were so good that most of them are
still with us: *Mimi, If I Love Again, The Song Is You,
Yesterdays, The Very Thought of You, I Get a Kick Out
of You, I'm in the Mood for Love, The Way You Look*

Tonight, and *Love Walked In*—among others. We play a game at my house nowadays in which one member of the company names a song of the 'thirties and the others must sing it with words and melody intact; or, as a variation, the challenger hums a few bars of a tune and the contestants must name it. Sounds simple and so it is, unless you happen to possess (as I do) a nasty great whacking list of such stumpers as *By the River Sainte Marie*, *In the Valley of the Moon*, *The Beat O' My Heart*, *A Melody from the Sky*, *It Looks Like Rain in Cherry-Blossom Lane*, and *Moonlight on the Colorado*—all well-known hits in the 'thirties. Even one of our most gifted tune-detectives lost a dollar on *The Beat O' My Heart* when he larcenously warbled it to the tune of *The Touch of Your Hand*.

Father and Bud were regular first-nighters, and so was I, when anyone invited me. Ladies and gentlemen dressed for the theatre in those times, not only on opening nights but every night, and although they generally went out to the lobby for a cigarette and a chat during intermission, there was none of the present mad scrambling into a neighboring bar for a quick one before the next act. People actually seemed willing and able to sit through an entire two-and-a-half-hour performance without a drink. Going to a first night was like going to an exceptionally well-dressed party, and the only two members of the audience I can recall who did not dress were the two drama critics, Heywood Broun, who always appeared to be wearing something that had been flung at him, and Richard Watts, who seemingly could not be parted from his "thousand-miler" blue shirt long enough to put on a dinner jacket.

My son and I lived in a small apartment with Anna Pines, the Black Panther, and Topsy, the Scotty, who were later succeeded by Rose Mitchelson, Sarah's daughter, and (on Topsy's demise) by Topper, a red cocker spaniel. Although we had our own home, our headquarters pretty much remained with Father and Bud—at Sag Harbor in the summer and the Algonquin in winter. Christmas was always a great occasion with the Case family. On Christmas Eve, Father held open house in the Algonk lobby with free refreshments for one and all, the only requirement being that everybody help trim the huge tree that brushed the ceiling in the corner between the Rose Room and the Oak Room. Great cartons of tree-trimmings—the same every year—were brought into the lobby, and Dennis King, or Vinton Freedley, or one of the Marx Brothers would teeter on the high ladder, placing the star at the top, while Gertrude Stein and Ina Claire and Peggy Wood, say, wrangled pleasantly about the disposal of ornaments below. There were so many people there that my particular grouping may be at fault; but all of those I have mentioned were usually present, and I particularly remember Gertrude Stein, one Christmas Eve, because of the grateful way she thanked Father for a pleasant evening. "If it hadn't been for the Algonquin tree-trimming," she told him sincerely, "I might never have met Gypsy Rose Lee!"

When the tree-trimming was over, each year, my son Guion and I went home; but only to return early Christmas morning, gift-laden, for our own family Christmas in the family's apartment at the Algonk. At this rite, Father properly became the focal point. He sat in his easy chair by the table in the window, wearing the expression of a ten-year-old boy waiting for goodies, and all of us fell over one another in our eagerness to give them to him.

In spite of his enthusiasm, he was not the easiest man to give presents to. He would never carry anything in his pockets that interfered with the "hang" of his clothes; so you could not give him a wallet, a cigar case, a lighter, or anything else that would clutter up his lean and graceful person. What he loved was things to wear, something he could put *on*. One Christmas, Bud and Germaine, those demon needlewomen, made him six pairs of tailored silk pajamas (Bud) and two tailored cashmere jackets, to wear while reading in bed (Germaine). Another Christmas, Bud actually made him six tailored shirts, which he never outwardly complained of; and Germaine tailored for him a handmade waistcoat.

I could not compete against these artists, nor did I want to. I gave Father things that could not be made at home —such as black silk evening socks from Charvet, and hats. Father was crazy about hats. One Christmas I gave him a Swiss number with a silver hatband and a "brush," and another year I gave him a black Homburg. Both of these hats were such successes that Doug Fairbanks borrowed them from Father repeatedly, and finally stole them altogether.

What Father failed to offer in scope, as far as Christmas presents went, he more than made up for in appreciation on Christmas morning. He always took a long time over opening each gift, first admiring in such detail the way it was wrapped that Bud and Germaine and I went crazy for weeks beforehand, trying to think up new tricks of gift-wrapping. I think I can say, with no false modesty, that I invented a hundred Christmas-wrapping gimmicks years before the department stores and "gift counselors" began to make a big production of pretty packages. I used *everything* on packages: Christmas tree balls, Christmas tree lights (with the battery concealed under ribbons, so that the lights lit up when the ribbon was pulled), wedding-cake dolls, penny whistles, gingerbread-men, fresh Burgundy carnations . . . anything that came in handy. One year I unearthed a box of discarded costume jewelry, and used that. No Christmas present could possibly be more appealing than when it is wrapped in violet-colored metallic paper bound with pink dime-store pearls; or enclosed in gold or silver paper, with a huge ten-cent rhinestone clip on top.

Father always handed around each prettily wrapped package to be exclaimed over by everyone, including whoever had given it to him, before he opened it. Then he would take out his thin gold pocketknife (the only object he ever carried, except a wafer-thin gold watch) and tidily slit the ends of the paper, being careful not to tear it. Then another happy interval of "Oh, Bud!"—or Oh, Margaret, or Guion, or Germaine, or Carroll or Josephine if my brother and his wife happened to be in town and were with us—as he drew out his gift. Christmas morning lasted a satisfactorily long time with us, for Father took the same itemized interest in the presents we all received as in his own. I remember him, one year, sitting in his new dressing gown and his new Charvet socks with a new muffler around his neck and his new Homburg on his head, raptly praising a pottery ash tray my son had made for me in school. The ash tray is beside me as I write, and I have just put out a cigarette in it.

Father was a very rewarding man to give clothes to, because, although neither a hypochondriac nor a dandy, he always took great care of his well-being and his looks. He never drank alcohol, almost never smoked until his after-dinner Corona, and, for a man in a sedentary profession, managed to get in a good deal of ice skating, dancing and horseback riding. His figure, posture and walk were, all of

his life, those of a young man. As far back as I can remember he had one ankle that cracked rhythmically when he walked, but this, with us, was more a means of identification than a suggestion of age. Nobody sitting in the family's apartment when Father got off the elevator had to guess that it was Father coming; the ankle cracked all the way down the corridor. It annoyed him slightly always to be thus pre-announced, and more than once he murmured plaintively that a man with a cracking ankle couldn't have any secrets at *all*.

Father was a little vain about his eyesight, which was so good that he never wore glasses, even for reading, until the last dozen or so years of his life, and then only after a picturesque struggle against them. I came into the family's apartment one day and found him standing at one end of the living room making violent faces at an oculist's chart pinned to the draperies at the other end, some thirty feet away. An eye doctor had told him that, by exercising the muscles of his eyes, he could avoid the use of eyeglasses indefinitely, and for quite a while afterward Father followed his instructions so actively that we worried for fear his face never would get back in shape again. Often in the middle of an otherwise charming conversation he would suddenly begin to revolve his eyeballs, or alternately stretch and narrow his lids, or dart his pupils from side to side, and it was only after we all insisted that he was beginning to look like a shifty gambler with an unfortunate tic that he gave up the exercises and bought a pair of glasses.

Possibly one reason Father was so fond of hats was that he looked younger with a hat on, owing to an extremely receding hairline. Douglas Fairbanks once bought him a toupée, and dared him to wear it into the Rose Room at lunchtime. Father did, and indignantly reported that it had caused no sensation whatever. "If those people were being polite," he complained, "you would think that at least *one* of 'em would have had the manners to faint dead away!" Because of his own lack of it, he admired a wealth of hair in others, especially women. In Florida, one time, I let my hair grow shoulder-length and sent Pa a snapshot of it.

"I like the increase in hair," he wrote me in reply, "for I may tell you now that I never knew how much I liked Bud's hair or yours until after it or they was or were gone —all cropped short. You never miss the water till a bad penny comes home to roost—*you* know. Bud's hair was so long and lovely; now from a back view I frequently mistake her for Fannie Ward or a date palm. With a little more frizzing and a couple of snakes, she could make Ringling Bros. Why in the name of Herpicide all women must have wavy, curly, or frizzy hair I don't know. There is no more straight hair.

"Suppose," Father's letter went on, "suppose all men got one idea, and all decided to be bald. Why, a bald head would cease to be a thing of beauty."

Sometime in the late nineteen-thirties, Father rather reluctantly opened a supper club in the Oak Room of the Algonquin. It was a practical business move, as the restaurant and night-club trade had been flourishing since repeal, but Father shied like a mustang from the notion of going into the night-club business. For one thing, a whole evening of drinking ice water from table to table was too much to contemplate, even for him, the champion hydropot of Forty-fourth Street; for another, he had done his bit of staying up all night, he said, in the old days with Jack Barrymore and Eugene Walter and Paul Armstrong, and he now planned to continue getting to bed at a decent hour.

To Bud and to his manager, John Martin, who were both in favor of the supper club, Father made it plain that they would have to see to the running of it, and that his only association with it would be to share in collecting the profits. Naturally, he did not stick wholly to his resolve; wherever people gathered, there Father was drawn, for he loved people as a hummingbird loves flowers, and the Algonquin Supper Club proved to be a crowded and popular place.

It was small and informal, with Cy Walter at the piano, Norbert Faconi playing violin, John Buckmaster (and later Eddie Mayehoff) doing comedy monologues, and Greta Keller singing Viennese, French and American songs. The paid entertainment was often supplemented by talent among the tables as Gladys Swarthout or Dennis King or whoever, hearing a familiar melody from Cy and Norbert, would start humming it and, with a little urging, sing it loud and clear. A moment I remember occurred one night when Walter Huston, who was living at the hotel, came in for supper after his performance in *Knickerbocker Holiday*. On an impulse, and without any announcement, he strolled from his table, leaned against the piano, and as Cy and Norbert softly played, sang to a suddenly hushed and enchanted room the wistful words of the *September Song*.

Standing there in an ordinary business suit, without makeup or costume or special lighting, he created a magic that hung in the air for a long moment after he finished, and then dissolved in a roar of applause and cheers. Stage people have a wonderful way of liking to go on working even after they leave a theatre, and when they can play to an audience like the one in the Algonk Supper Club, mostly made up of other stage people, they will cheerfully work all night for the pure joy of it.

I was by way of being a "cat" musically, although the term was little known in those days, and sometimes Cy Walter, Alec Wilder and Mitch Miller would let me sit in on jam sessions, or on rehearsals of an octette Alec and Mitch had formed with Walter Gross, Jimmy Carroll and five other musician's musicians for the purpose of recording Alec's compositions. These were rather recondite works for clarinet, flute, oboe, bass, bassoon, base clarinet, harpsichord and drums, and they had titles like "His First Long Pants," "Her Old Man Was Suspicious," and "The House Detective Registers." But their wonderful, pure-jazz rhythm plus the clear elegance of oboe and flute made them sound unlike anything else, except possibly Debussy dreaming of a juke joint, and they were dearer to Alec's heart than his later popular successes, "The King's Horses" and "It's So Peaceful in the Country." The oboeist in the octette was Mitch Miller, now the bearded genius who, as head of the "popular" department of Columbia Records, is the discoverer of such recording stars as Rosemary Clooney and Johnnie Ray, among many others. Mitch was clean-shaven then, and the most prosperous member of the octette, rushing regularly from studio to studio to broadcast with orchestras ranging from Benny Goodman's to Toscanini's. He used to explain his success by pointing out that pianists and fiddlers were a dime a dozen, but a good man on the oboe was hard to find, and he further remarked that he owed it all to an incident in his extreme youth.

"When I went out for the school band all the other kids were ahead of me in picking out their instruments," said

Mitch. "By the time I got there, the only thing left was the oboe."

Life, although not all supper clubs and jam sessions, continued to be full of variety. I would spend the morning at the typewriter, lunch at the Algonk with Father or other friends, do research or interviews in the afternoon, then hurry home to dress for a large evening at dinner or the theatre—with my son, if he was home on vacation, or with another date if he was at Lawrenceville. I had no steady beau, for I was following Father's advice, written to me while I was getting a divorce in Florida.

"You want to know what I think of R.B.," my sire had written, concerning some hovering swain; "a gentleman, obviously, and, I think, a fine chap. But for the luvvagawd and the sake of your old man, take it easy. Don't go nosing around new traps before you've got your hind leg free from the last one."

Father, a sixth-generation Episcopalian originally out of Framingham, Massachusetts, had his own ideas about marriage and divorce. He himself was married twice and widowed both times, but he hated all illiberal views on divorce, or on anything else. One day, he was chatting at lunch with a rather impressive dame when a much-married actress came into the Rose Room. The lady with Father stared at her, then lifted her eyebrows.

"She is beautiful, of course, and very talented, but she is a divorced woman," she said. "Somehow I cannot wholly admire a divorced woman, can you, Mr. Case?"

I was present, and I saw Father bite back the words that sprang to his lips. What he said was merely, "Well, my wife was a divorced woman when she married me, and my daughter is a divorced woman now, so you can scarcely

233

expect me to agree with you. *Good*-bye, so nice to see you! Come, Margaret."

Father, believing that age had little relation to looks or charm, was also inclined to be testy toward mature ladies who remarked of an actress, "Oh, I remember seeing her on the stage when I was a lit-tul girl!" He would give these persons a long look and murmur, "It's possible. I believe the actress you mention was carried onstage in her mother's arms for her first appearance."

My escorts, in the evenings, varied all the way from fellow writers who took me to Bleeck's to play the match-game to real fancy Racquet Club boys, and one of the fanciest was one whom I shall call Willie, for that was his name. Willie was a miraculous dancer and a magnificent squire. When you went out with Willie you got, not one gardenia corsage, but three in the course of the evening. The first was delivered to your apartment while you were dressing, the second arrived at the dinner table as you were about to leave the restaurant for the theatre, and the third replacement was waiting on your table at the night club after the theatre. A girl was supposed to discard the old corsage before pinning on the new, but I could never bear to do this, and was consequently hung with gardenias from chin to hemline by the end of an evening.

One incident about Willie I later made into a "casual" for *The New Yorker*, but that was long ago, and I am going to take the risk of repeating it because I like it so much. One night in a supper club, after several months of Willie's lavish treatment, he said to me, "Maggie, why don't we get married?" I was astonished and must have looked it, for Willie pressed his point.

"We get along fine together, we like all of the same

things," he went on. "We both like music, and the theatre, and dancing, and horses——"

"Horses!" I exclaimed. "Willie, *I* don't like horses. I'm scared to death of horses. I hate horses!"

Willie eyed me incredulously, and then slapped the table in disgust.

"Well!" he cried indignantly. "Why didn't you tell me that sooner? I wouldn't have gone to all this *trouble!*"

Willie never took me out again.

In the nineteen-thirties I sold my first piece to *The Saturday Evening Post* and lightheartedly blew most of the check on taking out a membership in the Embassy Club, a popular dancing spot on East Fifty-seventh Street where I loved to give parties. The Embassy was a large room, entered by way of a wide staircase which was fine for showing off your latest gown. This staircase was surely never the scene of more emotional turmoil than on the night I invited Douglas Fairbanks, Jr. and his recent bride, Joan Crawford, to a party.

I had met Miss Crawford only once, one day when Doug brought her, as his fiancée, to lunch at the Algonquin with his mother, Beth. She was wearing a sleeveless, backless, California sun dress, not exactly the quiet attire one might expect from a bride-to-be lunching in town with her future mother-in-law, and she seemed very nervous. However, she was beautiful and very attentive to Doug; from my own table I couldn't help noticing the way she kept buttering pieces of roll and pressing them on him. I learned afterward that she considered him underweight and wanted to feed him up.

The Fairbankses were a little late, this night at the

Embassy, and my party were already seated when the headwaiter came to me and said, "Mr. and Mrs. Fairbanks have arrived."

"Good," I said. "Ask them to join us."

"I am sorry, they ask to see you," said the headwaiter.

"Well, *I'm* sorry, but I can't leave my guests. Ask Mr. and Mrs. Fairbanks to join us, please."

He went away, and presently Douglas arrived, looking worried. "Gee, Maggie," he murmured to me, after he had been introduced to the others, "I hate to ask you, but Joan is in the powder room and I think she needs you."

Imagining all possible disasters from a fainting fit to a broken slipper heel, I hurried up to the powder room at the top of the grand staircase. Joan, looking dazzling but dejected, sat in a small chair, doing the nearest thing to wringing her hands. She looked up as I entered and said to me these words: "I can't! I can't, I just can't! I *can't* walk down that long staircase in front of all those people!"

Restraining an impulse to belt her one, I tried reasoning and cajolery, to no avail. "No, no, no," she insisted, and finally she whispered, "Go get Douglas."

I sent Douglas to her, and of course, the handsome pair made a magnificent entrance down the staircase a few moments later, with every eye in the room on them. I do not say that Joan planned all of this deliberately; I think that, at that time, she was genuinely shy. But I also believe that her sense of theatre perhaps subconsciously directed the whole scene, including the slight excitement and well-timed delay, so that when she did come down the stairs on the arm of her new husband, no head in that room would be turned in any other direction. From that moment, Miss Crawford's steadily ascending career has never surprised me.

Nor has Douglas's, for that matter. He is a little too grand for the likes of me these days, now that the Queen comes to dine at his London house, but my recollections of him are all lively and spiced with adventure. One of my later encounters with him, long after he and Joan were divorced, was positively Graustarkian, and it would never had happened were it not for the solemn truth that you get what you give in this life, a favor done is a future insured, and bread cast upon the waters returns as croissants and jam.

One day Clay Morgan, a press agent for the National Broadcasting Company, telephoned me to say that NBC had imported a French singer named Jean Sablon who didn't speak a word of English, but knowing I spoke French, Mr. Morgan thought that Sablon might make a good subject for a *New Yorker* Profile. *New Yorker* writers were cool to Profile suggestions from press agents, and in any case M. Sablon turned out to be too young to provide enough material for a Profile. I wrote nothing about him in *The New Yorker*. However, I did meet him, and after one look at the young Frenchman (whose masculine beauty is known to all by now), I untiringly devoted myself for several months to keeping him diverted in a strange land, talking French with him, seeing that he met French-speaking friends of mine, having him for cocktails, and otherwise striving to make his path less rough. The work was arduous but I enjoyed it, and as I say, I was rewarded. That summer at Sag Harbor I was called to the phone one morning, and it was Clay Morgan announcing that the French Line, for which he also directed publicity, had invited a group of journalists to spend a month in France as guests of the *Bureau de Tourisme*, sailing and returning on the new *Normandie*. In view of my selfless efforts on behalf of Jean Sablon, Mr. Morgan added, he was prepared to do me a good turn; would I care to go along?

Would I! I had my bags packed before the telephone stopped vibrating and, leaving my son Guion with Frankie and Bud at Sag, took off in a rosy cloud.

The office of the French Tourist Bureau in New York informed me that the only service requested from the voyaging journalists was that we each, on our return, write an article for an American publication stating that we liked France and that it was a nice place, or words to that effect. I had a qualm. "But I already love France," I told them. "I don't have to travel six thousand miles on the cuff to make that statement!" Never mind, they said courteously, come along anyway and see if I didn't find even some new things to like. I was the only unattached woman in a group consisting of John R. Tunis and his wife, Richard Dunlap of the *Herald-Tribune* and his wife, and a newspaperman named George with *his* wife, Mary. I shall always remember Mary as the least impassioned sight-seer I have ever known. It was her first trip to Europe, and at every town we visited—Paris, and all through Normandy and Brittany and down to the Riviera—Mary's first and only heartfelt inquiry was, "Where can I find a hairdresser?"

My own mind was on higher things, such as a slight but promising romance with one of the extremely presentable Frenchmen who escorted our party, whose tender pronouncement one moonlit evening in Vichy still lives in

my heart. I note it here in the original French, since it loses in translation.

Strolling along the Promenade on this enchanted night, the two of us stopped at one of the *buvettes* which dispense the mineral waters of the region, and Etienne handed me a cup of boiling-hot *eau de Chomel*.

"*J'ai quelque chose à vous dire,*" he murmured thrillingly.

I looked up at him over the cup of water, the stars reflected in my eyes. "*Eh bien, dites,*" I whispered.

"*N'oubliez jamais,*" he declared ringingly, "*de soigner vos intestins!*"

From Vichy our group returned for a few days more in Paris and then took the Golden Arrow, the crack Riviera train, to Antibes. Something or other delayed me in joining the others for dinner in the restaurant car, and as I hurried alone through the swaying corridors from car to car, I bumped into a tall figure smoking a cigarette in the twilight on one of the leaping platforms. After an exchange of "*pardons*" I started to go on, but peered again through the dusk, the figure peered at me, and "Maggie!" he shouted, and "Douglas!" I shrieked. Sure enough, it was our hero, Doug Fairbanks Jr., on his way to Monte Carlo.

There is always something wonderful about running into an old American friend in Europe, and it's even better when the old friend turns out to be Douglas. He dined with us that evening, speaking fluent French to the Frenchmen and rather British English to the Americans, and after dinner he and I repaired to my stateroom with a supply of hock-and-seltzer and had a long, refreshing gab far into the night. The train arrived early next morning at Antibes, where the usual welcoming committee of

Mayor and Tourist Bureau officials were lined up to receive our group; and surely no welcoming committee was ever given such a turn, as our party descended and the train started to pull out of the station. There was a rushing sound and a shrill protest from the guard, and young Mr. Fairbanks arrived at a gallop on the car steps with his arms full of flowers (presumably swiped from the vases in the restaurant car), which he proceeded to toss at us with one hand while he hung onto the now speeding train with the other. Our last view of him as the Golden Arrow hurtled down the tracks toward Monte Carlo was a wild silhouette of outflung arms and legs and blown kisses until somebody, probably the guard, yanked him out of sight.

It was good to have that gay memory of the south of France that year, because from Antibes we went to Biarritz, where my chief recollection is a sad one. One day I climbed to the top of an old ruined tower at Hendaye, on the Spanish border, with the Mayor of Biarritz, a tall, muscular, fierce-looking Basque named Irigoyen. Looking across into Spain, we could see the spurts of flame and hear the gunfire of the Spanish War. "It is coming for all of us," said M. Irigoyen in a low voice. I turned toward this big tough guy, and saw that the tears were running down his cheeks.

When I got back to America I wrote a piece for *Vogue*, saying that France was okay. It was a small return for a magnificent trip, but the Tourist Bureau seemed satisfied, and several readers wrote in, agreeing with me. There was one great difference, I found, in writing for the *New Yorker* and writing for other magazines: *New Yorker* readers don't write letters. Readers of *Vogue, Good House-*

keeping, SatEvePost and *Ladies Home Journal* sent me letters by the pack, approving or violently condemning, and one treasured customer in the state of Oregon went further than that; every Christmas for several years she sent me a great box of evergreen boughs, holly and pine cones, and every Thanksgiving a carton of homemade jams and jellies. *New Yorker* readers, with one exception, had no such cozy impulses. The exception, oddly enough, was the clergy.

On the day war was declared in Europe, September 3, 1939, I wrote a *New Yorker* "casual" called "Come-uppance for an Infidel" which truthfully described how I had wanted to go to church on that day for solace and reassurement, but could find no church in New York open because it was "out of season." This piece brought me letters from ministers all over the country, saying mainly that if I had tried *their* church I would have found no such fancy nuances. Even the celebrated Dr. Sargent of New York's St. Bartholomew's wrote inviting me, not only to church by way of his own private entrance, but for a swim in the new pool recently installed in St. Bartholomew's basement.

Preparing to acknowledge these letters, I came up against a problem of etiquette. Nearly all of the clergymen had signed themselves merely by their given names and surnames, with no clue as to whether they should be addressed as "Dear Mr. Soandso" or "Dear Dr. Soandso." What to do? What else but consult my friend, Emily Post? I wrote to her, posing the question, and her reply had all of her customary wisdom and quiet wit.

"Dear Mrs. Harriman," she wrote, "A clergyman is addressed as 'Mister' unless he is a Doctor of Divinity. However," she added pithily, "if you are in doubt as to his degree, may I suggest that you will never hurt a clergy-man's feelings by addressing him as 'Doctor.' "

Another slightly edgy public response came about after a chance meeting, on Madison Avenue, with that small lavender-haired dynamo known as Edna Woolman Chase, editor of *Vogue*.

"You always look so chic, dear," she said when we had chatted a moment. "Is that little frock a Balmain?"

"A Balmain!" I hooted. "This little frock is strictly a Lord and Taylor Budget Shop original, priced twenty-nine ninety-five."

That did it. When I added that I spent less than a thousand dollars a year on clothes, Mrs. Chase suggested promptly that I do a piece for *Vogue* on how to dress according to that budget. "We'll illustrate it with photographs of you in your own clothes, so come over to the studio on Monday to have pictures made," she said. "Wear what you have on, and bring a change."

The photographic sitting was presided over by my namesake, Miss Margaret Case, and she seemed a little less staggered by my chic than Mrs. Chase had been. After one glance, she tossed my clothes on a chair in the dressing room and hastily borrowed a dress and hat from another *Vogue* editor to deck me out in. This struck me as being insincere.

However, who was I to complain? My piece was truthful, anyway. After a careful reckoning I was even able to call it "How to Dress on $998.00 a Year" (yes, it could be done in those days), but M. F. Agha, the demon art editor, didn't like the looks of that decimal point in type, so the piece appeared under the title of "How to dress on $1000 a Year." The piece was ill-starred from the beginning. Unfortunately, in stressing the importance of accessories,

I happened to mention in the article that my father had given me a string of pearls and a fur coat. American womanhood retorted in a body, as follows:

"*Well!* If *my* father had given me a string of pearls and a fur coat, it would have been a nice *start* toward a thousand-dollar wardrobe!"

The repercussions in my own family were almost worse. "Where did *you* learn so much about clothes?" demanded my stepmother, a well-dressed woman.

"From you," I answered sweetly.

Father was even sterner. "Where did you ever learn the value of a dollar, finally?" he inquired.

"I guess from being without one," I said meekly.

There was a great shaking of heads all round, and I wished I had never written the damn piece.

Actually, Father had a right to be astonished by any thrifty admonishments publicly offered by me. He had held a low opinion of my financial ability ever since my eighteenth birthday when he presented me with ten shares of American Tel & Tel (or some such sturdy stock), and I instantly sold it to Bushie, the Algonquin telephone operator, for ready cash. Father was angry with Bushie and me about that deal, and even when he calmed down he said bitterly, "If my telephone operator is smarter than my daughter, she deserves to have the stock."

Father never actually understood how I came to be self-supporting as a writer. "You make a lot of money, but you *spend* it!" he would say, when I brought him a birthday gift. All through the 'thirties and into the 'forties, he always sent me his twenty-dollar fee for being a member of the Board of the Chemical Bank. In the early days it was a twenty-dollar gold piece. Later, when Roosevelt called the gold in, it was a check for twenty-five dollars. I tried to tell Father that I didn't really need it.

"It's a tradition," said Father, "just the way you put a silver dollar in Guion's stocking every Christmas."

He had me there. I have put a silver dollar into the toe of my son's stocking every Christmas since he was born, and I never fail to slip a silver dollar, every Christmas, into the stocking of Sheila, my son's wife, and the stockings of Lee and Hilary, my grandchildren.

They don't need it. It's just a tradition, as Father said. Father, like me, was fond of family traditions, but often irritated by them. He wanted his children to behave like Cases, but when they did, he sometimes found it intolerable. "Good God," he moaned, one time when he found me sulking in my room on account of a fancied offense, "stop acting like your Aunt Jenny!"

No two people as definite in personality as my father and I could maintain a lifelong affection without minor clashes; and Father and I sometimes clashed. One time was when Father's book, "Tales of a Wayward Inn," was published. I was in Florida, and I sent Father a long, affectionate telegram of congratulation and praise.

He replied with a crisp note, via ordinary mail, pointing out the evils of extravagance, and the fact that night rates were available at all Western Union offices. This message so cut me to the quick that I sent Father a long telegram of frosty apology. I sent it Collect.

Father's reproofs were usually more gentle and more subtle. One time he took a real dislike to a beau of mine, a blue-eyed young man who wore a small mustache, a fancy hat, and a wing collar with a bow tie. Father smoldered in silence about this apparition, even after he and Bud took off on a trip to California.

Presently a box arrived for me, from the Farmers' Market in Los Angeles. Obviously from Father, even if his name had not been written on the return address. The box contained a large pink china cat, wearing a fancy hat and a necktie. I put the cat on my mantelpiece and immediately got into a state of nerves. Every time I looked at it, or even passed by it, it reminded me of something or somebody just out of my mind's reach. It took me some time to realize that this china cat was a copy of my beau— blue popeyes, fancy hat, necktie and all. I could never look at my beau again without seeing him as the china cat. So that was, quite properly, the end of that romance.

Father had a gift for bringing things to the proper conclusion, without saying a single word. But sometimes he was terribly articulate.

"Get on a plane and come home!" he said to me once, calling from Sag Harbor to Florida. "The papers and the radio say this hurricane is about to hit Florida, and I want you to get out of there and come home!"

"Father," I said, "nobody here is worried, we're all boarded up, and besides everybody thinks the hurricane is going to blow out to sea. . . ."

"Margaret?" said Father anxiously, "I have to hang up now. The roof just blew off the bathhouse."

That was the famous hurricane of 1938 which did not blow out to sea, but blew up north and devastated Long Island. We lost our bathhouse at Sag, and part of our sea wall, and a few beautiful oak trees.

"And I was worried about *you*, and the perils of that Florida sunshine!" said Father a little bitterly, when it was all over.

"I'm glad you got back all right," he said, giving me a great hug.

* Chapter 10 *

MY stepmother, Bud, died after a long illness, in February, 1946. My father then made the two most tragic remarks I have ever heard.

"Bud had such wonderful teeth, and such strong, thick hair," he said, "wouldn't you have thought that they could have given her some strength when she needed it?"

And then he said, "Caroline died in February, too."

Father didn't seem to care much about living after he lost Bud. He died of a coronary occlusion four months later, in June.

Rusty, the Algonquin cat, deliberately stopped living ten days after Father's death. Rusty was a great marmalade cat in the prime of life—a famous cat who drank his cream from a champagne glass at the Algonquin bar, and who grandly rode the elevator to the tenth floor and no farther, because that was where he lived. After Bud and Father died, Rusty stopped eating, even though Germaine tempted him with cream and liver and fancy fish. Finally we took him to Dr. Kinney, where he simply laid down and died.

"You don't often hear of a cat dying of grief," said Dr. Kinney, "but this cat did."

Germaine and I took Rusty down to Sag Harbor and buried him in Sarah's garden, under the marigold bed.

Here is a true ghost story that happened to me and my brother Carroll and his wife, Josephine, one sunny day at Sag Harbor, the summer after Father and Bud died.

We had been staying at Sag while appraisers went through the house sorting furniture, linens, silver and otherwise attending to the details of settling an estate. Now, on Sunday, they had gone, leaving us alone, and we brought some cushions out onto the side lawn and sat there, lazily talking. It was one of those bright, still afternoons when there is no sound except the light slap of water against the shore and the drone of your own voices.

Suddenly and unmistakably the screen door at the front of the house banged, and Father's famous ankle went cracking down the flagstone path toward the beach. We all heard it.

I guess it was half a minute before I said, "Did you hear that?"

"Yes," said Carroll.

"But there's nobody in the house," whispered Jo.

"Maybe it's Frank Corwin from the village, or somebody from the Cummings' looking for us," Carroll sensibly suggested. But there was no car in the driveway, nobody had walked past us, and nobody had walked up from the beach. Most of all, nobody's ankle cracked like Frankie's.

We went through the house and down to the beach, yoo-hooing and calling, "Is anybody here?" Nobody was there. Back at the house I called up the Cummings, our

nearest neighbors, who lived a quarter of a mile up the beach. No, said Mrs. Cummings, nobody from her place had been at our place today. Slightly shaken, we went back and sat down on our cushions in the sun again.

The next thing that happened, startling as it was, came almost as an anticlimax. Sitting where we were, we happened to be facing the back porch and, above it, Bud's room which we ourselves had closed and dust-sheeted the day before, after the departure of the appraisers.

In the middle of whatever one of us was saying, another unmistakable sound jerked our heads in a single direction.

A window in Bud's room had gone *up*.

This time we hurtled into the house in a body, searching and calling through every room. There was no one there, of course. The house was empty, as we knew it was.

But in Bud's room, where we had closed all the windows, one window was open.

We can't explain any of this, Carroll, Jo and I. We only know that we saw it happen.

Now, ten years later, it begins to make sense to me. After all, perhaps two people like Father and Bud, who spent thirty happy summers at Sag Harbor, do not leave Sag Harbor all at once.

Yesterday I went to lunch at the Algonquin. It was a horrid February day, raining, sleeting and trying to snow, with a big wind howling down every block, and I was glad to get off my wet coat and wet boots, and check them.

In the Rose Room I was interested only in the menu, until a familiar voice addressed me. It was the waiter.

"How's da Margaret?" he inquired.

"Nick!" I said, "What are you doing down here?"

It was a question that Nick's English was not capable of answering, at least not in words. By some kind of sign language he told me that he had been promoted from room waiter to restaurant waiter. I congratulated him and we shook hands, and then Nick, as I knew he would, spoke the famous words: " 'S'nice day today!" he offered.

I looked at this man who had served my father for thirty years, who had brought him ten thousand breakfasts always with the same cheery news: " 'S'nice day today!" Whether it was raining, or snowing, or sleeting.

I thought of the storm outside. It was raining and snowing and sleeting. My feet were wet, and the curl was out of my hair. Nick was waiting for my order, but I didn't give it right away.

I said, "What did you say, Nick?"

He said, " 'S'nice day today!"

"You are so right, Nick," I said. "It's a *nice* day, today!"